7 Steps to Bible Skills

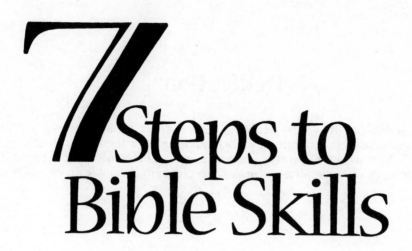

Dorothy Hellstern

HENSLEY
PUBLISHING

Dedication

I dedicate this book to the young people in several churches in Kansas and Oklahoma who participated in this program in its beginning, and to the students at Oklahoma Christian School whose eagerness, diligence, and achievement encouraged me to continue with the effort to make the program available to others.

7 Steps to Bible Skills

ISBN 1-56322-029-6

7 Steps to Bible Skills

Table of Contents

ABOUT PHOTOCOPYING THIS BOOK

Some people who would never walk into a store and shoplift a book may think nothing of photocopying the same book. The results are the same. Both acts are wrong.

First Timothy 5:17-18 instructs us to give the laborer his wages, specifically those who labor in the Word and doctrine. As a publisher, we have a moral as well as a legal responsibility to see that our authors receive fair compensation for their efforts. Many of them depend on the income from the sale of these books as their livelihood. So, for that matter, do the artists, printers, and numerous other people who work to make these books available to you.

Please help us abide by the laws of both God and man by discouraging those who would photocopy any portion of this book in lieu of purchase.

WE WANT TO KNOW WHAT YOU THINK ABOUT THIS STUDY!

Please share your comments or suggestions with us at:

editorial@hensleypublishing.com

Toll Free Ordering: 800.288.8520
Fax: 918.664.8562
Phone: 918.664.8520

Order Online for Extra Savings!
www.hensleypublishing.com

HENSLEY
PUBLISHING

6116 E 32nd St
Tusa Ok 74135

Introduction

How many different kinds of books have you read in your lifetime? If you're like most people, you've probably read many different kinds — from schoolbooks that teach you, to storybooks filled with fun and adventure.

The most important book you will ever read, however, is the Bible. It isn't like any other book you'll ever read. It's one of the oldest books ever written, and it has about 40 different authors. From the earliest to the latest, the writing took over 1,000 years.

Why is the Bible so important? Because it tells us about God, the Creator of the universe. When God created human beings, He made us special. He made us in His own image. Since He is spirit, He made us spirit. Then He put our spirit into a body and gave us a mind with which to think and plan and ask questions. He gave us special ability to talk with Him and to know Him.

God knew that we would have many questions:

WHO AM I?
WHO MADE THIS WORLD I LIVE IN?
WHAT IS THE PURPOSE OF IT ALL?
WHAT IS THE FUTURE GOING TO BE
  FOR THE WORLD?

God chose three ways to show Himself to man:

IN CREATION
The heavens declare the glory of God; and the firmament showeth his handiwork. (Psalm 19:1)

IN HIS SON, JESUS CHRIST
Jesus . . . said, "He that believeth on me, believeth not on me, but on Him that sent me. And he that seeth me seeth Him that sent me." (John 12:44-45)

IN HIS WORD, THE BIBLE
I have given them thy word . . . . Sanctify them through thy truth: thy word is truth . . . . Neither pray I for these alone, but for them also which shall believe on me through their word . . . . (John 17:14-20)

By reading the Bible we can learn the answers to our questions. We can get to know who God is and what He's like. The Bible tells us the story of God's love. It tells us about the beginning of sin and how sin separated us from our Creator. Since death is the penalty for sin, every man would have to die to pay for his sins. But God loved us so much that He planned a way to have those sins paid for by His very own Son, Jesus Christ. Now it's possible for us, once again, to walk and talk with our God. And, best of all, we can live with Him forever.

Because the Bible is so important, all of us should become Bible students. A Bible student wants to know for himself what the

Bible says. He wants to learn how to use its teachings every day. Studying the Bible takes time and skill. To learn these skills, we must have teaching and practice. That's what this study program is all about.

This book is your Student Workbook for *7 Steps to Bible Skills*. Look at the Table of Contents. You'll see that the book is divided into seven units called "Steps." You'll be taking those steps as you follow your Workbook. Each step will lead you farther along the pathway of a skillful Bible student. It's going to be an exciting journey — one that you'll never forget.

WORDS TO KNOW To be a good Bible student, you must know the meanings of some new words. Don't let these new words hold you back. This sign will guide you to the meanings you need to learn. Be faithful in following the signs. You'll find yourself growing stronger and stronger as you go.

Memorizing some of the scripture verses will also help you be a better Bible student. Look for this lamp and memorize the verse. Let the scriptures be a "lamp unto your feet" as you go.

HIGH CLIMBERS There are always a few travelers who want to do more than just walk along the pathway. They want to climb up the mountains to get a better view. Or, perhaps they just like the excitement of the climb. If you're a High Climber, then look for these mountains as you go. Accept the challenge. See how high you can climb. Even if you don't get to the highest peak, you'll have the fun of reaching for the top.

PROGRESS RECORD FOR _____

Keep your own record of achievement by coloring the footsteps as you pass them, the mountains as you climb them, and the memory verses as you learn them.

STEPS PASSED	MOUNTAINS CLIMBED	MEMORY VERSES LEARNED
Step 1		☐ Ps. 119:105
		☐ II Tim. 2:15
Step 2		☐ Ps. 119:11
		☐ Isa. 40:8
Step 3		☐ Mt. 5:17
		☐ Mk. 13:31
Step 4		☐ II Tim. 3:16-17
		☐ Ps. 119:130
		☐ Ps. 119:89
Step 5		☐ Jn. 8:31b-32
		☐ Heb. 11:6
		☐ Rom. 15:4
Step 6		☐ Ps. 119:133
		☐ Rom. 12:2
		☐ Lk. 2:52
Step 7		☐ Lk. 11:28b

Step 1

Books of the Bible

BOOKS OF THE BIBLE AND HOW TO SAY THEM

OLD TESTAMENT		NEW TESTAMENT	
Genesis	*JEN e sis*	Matthew	*MATH ū*
Exodus	*EK sō dus*	Mark	*mark*
Leviticus	*le VIT i kus*	Luke	*loōk*
Numbers	*NUM berz*	John	*jon*
Deuteronomy	*DOO ter ON uh mē*		
		Acts	*akts*
Joshua	*JOSH ū uh*	Romans	*RŌ munz*
Judges	*JUJ iz*	I Corinthians	*kuh RIN thi unz*
Ruth	*ROOTH*	II Corinthians	
		Galatians	*guh LĀ shunz*
I Samuel	*SAM ū el*	Ephesians	*i FĒ shunz*
II Samuel		Philippians	*fi LIP e unz*
I Kings	*kings*	Colossians	*kuh LOSH unz*
II Kings			
I Chronicles	*KRON i k'lz*	I Thessalonians	*thes uh LŌ ne unz*
II Chronicles		II Thessalonians	
		I Timothy	*TIM uh thē*
Ezra	*EZ ruh*	II Timothy	
Nehemiah	*NĒ uh MĪ uh*	Titus	*TĪ tus*
Esther	*ES ter*	Philemon	*fī LĒ mun*
Job	*jōbe*	Hebrews	*HĒ brooz*
Psalms	*sahlmz*	James	*jāmz*
Proverbs	*PRO verbz*	I Peter	*PĒ ter*
Ecclesiastes	*i KLĒ zi AS tēz*	II Peter	
Song of Solomon	*SOL o mun*	I John	*jon*
		II John	
Isaiah	*ī ZĀ uh*	III John	
Jeremiah	*JER e MĪ uh*		
Lamentations	*LAM un TĀ shunz*	Jude	*jood*
Ezekiel	*i ZĒ ke ehl*	Revelation	*rev uh LĀ shun*
Daniel	*DAN yehl*		
Hosea	*hō ZĀ uh*		
Joel	*JŌ ehl*		
Amos	*Ā mus*		
Obadiah	*ō buh DĪ uh*		
Jonah	*JŌ nuh*		
Micah	*MĪ kuh*		
Nahum	*NĀ hūme*		
Habakkuk	*huh BAK uk*		
Zephaniah	*ZEF uh NĪ uh*		
Haggai	*HAG e ī*		
Zechariah	*ZEK uh RĪ uh*		
Malachi	*MAL uh kī*		

HIGH CLIMBERS

Learn to spell as many of the Books of the Bible as you possibly can.

10

Books of the Bible

Many people won't use their Bible for study because they don't know how to find the scriptures they want to read. This may be because they never learned where each book of the Bible is located. This skill, then, should be the first one for a Bible student to learn. It won't take very long. You may already have memorized them.

To complete STEP 1, you must be able to say the books of the Bible in order, slowly. You must not get confused or leave any of them out. Saying them fast, in a sort of "sing-song" way, is all right if it's the only way you can remember them. However, this won't help you as much in finding scriptures. If you need to start all the way back at the beginning and say the list each time you want to find a book, it will be too slow. You won't want to do it.

The best way to memorize the list is to begin by learning the correct pronunciation of each book. Study the list of books on page 10. It tells you how to say each name. As you sound out each name softly to yourself, listen to the sound of it. Say each one over and over until you're sure you're saying it correctly. Then, begin memorizing one small part of the list at a time. The pronunciation list has been marked for you in small groups. Practice the first five books of the Old Testament until you can say them easily. Then add the next three. Practice the first eight books until you know exactly where each one comes and can say them correctly. Now add the six double books. Continue until you can say the entire Old Testament list without a mistake. Then work on the New Testament books in the same way.

It's best to work in a quiet place where you can think. It also helps to work with someone else. Ask a friend to listen to you say your list. Then listen to your friend try to say the list. Hearing the names said over and over helps you keep them in your memory. If you must study alone, practice by opening your Bible to any book. Try to name the book that comes before and the one that comes after it.

TO TAKE THIS STEP —
Learn to say the books of the Bible in order with confidence.

A LAMP UNTO MY FEET

Thy word is a lamp unto my feet, and a light unto my path. (Psalm 119:105)

Step 2

Arrangement of the Bible

ARRANGEMENT OF THE BIBLE

OLD TESTAMENT (39 books)		NEW TESTAMENT (27 books)	
Books of the Law: *(5 books)*	Genesis Exodus Leviticus Numbers Deuteronomy	**The Gospels:** *(4 books)*	Matthew Mark Luke John
Books of History: *Theocracy* *(3 books)*	Joshua Judges Ruth	**Book of History:** *(1 book)*	Acts of the Apostles
Monarchy *(6 books)*	I Samuel II Samuel I Kings II Kings I Chronicles II Chronicles	**The Epistles:** By Paul *(13 books)*	Romans I Corinthians II Corinthians Galatians Ephesians Philippians Colossians I Thessalonians II Thessalonians I Timothy II Timothy Titus Philemon
Post Exile *(3 books)*	Ezra Nehemiah Esther		
Books of Poetry: *(5 books)*	Job Psalms Proverbs Ecclesiastes Song of Solomon	General *(8 books)*	Hebrews James I Peter II Peter I John II John III John Jude
Books of Prophecy: Major Prophets *(5 books)*	Isaiah Jeremiah Lamentations Ezekiel Daniel	**Book of Prophecy:** *(1 book)*	Revelation
Minor Prophets *(12 books)*	Hosea Joel Amos Obadiah Jonah Micah Nahum Habakkuk Zephaniah Haggai Zechariah Malachi		

HIGH CLIMBERS

Learn everything in italics on this chart. Be able to place major events of Bible history in proper divisions.

Arrangement of the Bible

If you can say the books of the Bible, you have just taken the first step on the pathway of a good Bible student. The next step is a little longer, but it will be very helpful to you. You're going to learn how this wonderful book is arranged.

If you wanted to arrange the books on a bookshelf, how would you do it? Would you arrange them by size, from the largest to the smallest? Would you arrange them by color? Or would you arrange them by subject? You could put the reading books together, then the math books and history books and science books. You're going to see that our Bible has been arranged, too. As a good Bible student, you need to know this arrangement. It will help you understand the Bible much better.

Our path is going to take us to a place where we can look over the whole Bible at one time. Study the chart on the Arrangement of the Bible. Then we'll take a walk through each book of the Bible to see what it is all about.

The word "Bible" comes from a Greek word which means "book." Because it's the most important book of all books, we sometimes call it "THE Book" or "THE Bible." The word Bible is always written with a capital letter because it is <u>sacred</u>. The best title of all is "Holy Bible."

Although it's thought of as *one* book, our Bible is really *many* books put together in one binding. These books were written by many different writers for many different purposes. All the Old Testament books were first written in the Hebrew language. Hebrew writing looks like this:

```
ישתה וכל מישורד עוד לא שיתה דאשר
להים ובישים לא ואבל מהבל חדת ועיתי
יה חל המהד חדל רחסד עתי לא י
```

The New Testament books were first written in the Greek language. Greek writing looks like this:

```
OCHNAIXMAΛ(I)
TOCEϵIΪΉΑΜʼHN
H XMAΛ(DTEΥCEN
```

Many people have <u>translated</u> these books into other languages over the years. Now almost any person anywhere in the world can read the Bible in his own language. Do you think you might someday be a Bible translator?

TWO TESTAMENTS

THE OLD TESTAMENT
39 BOOKS

THE NEW TESTAMENT
27 BOOKS

The books of the Bible are divided into two main parts. These parts are called *testaments*. The word "testament" has almost the same meaning as the word "covenant." A *covenant* is an agreement between two people or two groups. When a covenant is made, each person pledges to do something for the other. They often pledge to honor each other and to be loyal to each other. Sometimes, each one does something to show the other that he really

WORDS TO KNOW

sacred (SĀ krid)– *belonging to or dedicated to God.*
translated (trans LĀT ed)– *changed from one language into another.*

means to keep his promise. Today, we do this by signing our name to a paper. The terms of the agreement are explained on this paper. In past time, gifts were often given. In some cases, a monument was built as a reminder of the covenant.

The testaments of the Bible refer to a covenant between God and man. The Old Testament was a covenant between God (called Jehovah) and His special people (called Israelites). The New Testament is a covenant between God and His Son, Jesus Christ. Jesus was the only person who was able to keep all the terms of the Old Testament covenant. That's what we mean when we say that He fulfilled the law. Then He gave His life on the cross to pay for *our* sins. When we believe that He did this for us, then we become "joint heirs" with Him. We're in Jesus; He's in the Father, and that makes us part of a *new* covenant. The Bible says this new covenant is much better than the old one.

In the Bible used by most people there are 39 books in the Old Testament and 27 in the New Testament. Add those two numbers. Did you get 66? That's how many books are in the entire Bible. The Roman Catholic Church uses a Bible which includes some other books called the *Apocrypha* (Uh POK ri fuh). In the Jewish scriptures, the 39 books of the Old Testament are rearranged and combined to make only 28 books, and there is no New Testament at all. In our study, we'll be using the 39 books of the Old Testament. The Apocrypha will be explained in Step 4.

TO TAKE THIS STEP —

Learn the divisions of the Bible. Be able to name the five big groups in Old and New Testament.

Learn how many books are in each division and be able to name them.

THE OLD TESTAMENT

The books in the Bible are all about God. They tell one story about how God has made Himself known to man. Many stories of the Old Testament seem strange to us, but we must remember that those early people were just beginning to learn about God. Although they failed many times, God kept on loving them and trying to help them. This is what the Old Testament is all about. When the Old Testament story ended, the world was in great trouble. God's people needed help, and they couldn't help themselves. So, God sent Jesus. The New Testament is His story.

BOOKS OF THE LAW

The Old Testament is divided into five groups. The first five books of the Bible make up the first group. These five books are called the *Books of the Law* because they contain the Law which God gave to Moses. It is believed that Moses wrote these books many centuries before the time of Christ. They include much history, but they are called Books of the Law to keep us from confusing them with other books of history. Also, the history in the

Books of the Law has much to do with the receiving of the Law. The Law was part of the covenant between God and the Hebrew people. You will hear and read much about the covenant as you study the Bible.

Sometimes this group of books is called by other names. It will be very helpful to you if you learn these names, too. You will see them often in your study of the Bible. Remember that they are all referring to the first five books of the Bible.

Pentateuch (PEN tuh took) — Greek for "five scrolls."
Torah (TŌ ruh) — Hebrew for "the Law."
Mosaic Law (Mō ZĀ ik) — another way to say "the Law of Moses."

GENESIS

Genesis tells about the beginning of all history because it tells the story of Creation. It tells how the human race began with Adam and Eve and how their disobedience brought the curse of sin on all human beings. But God began immediately to prepare the way for man to be saved from this curse.

Great events took place during the first centuries of human history. There was a Great Flood. Noah and his family and the animals he took into the ark with him were the only living things that didn't drown.

You can read the story of the Tower of Babel, when man foolishly tried to reach God through his own efforts.

Later, you read about the beginning of a special race of people. Genesis follows the lives of Abraham and his family. God called Abraham and made a covenant with him. The covenant was made again with each generation — Isaac, Jacob, Joseph. When Genesis ends, the family has moved to Egypt to escape a famine in their own land.

EXODUS

Exodus continues the story of the Hebrews. They're now called Israelites, or Children of Israel. When they went to Egypt, they were a family of about 70 people. After 400 years, they had grown to be a large nation. This made the kings of Egypt afraid of them. So they made the Israelites slaves and used them to build large cities. But God sent a man named Moses to take them out of Egypt. This story is filled with mighty **miracles** which God performed for the Israelites.

During their journey out of Egypt, the Israelites camped at Mt. Sinai. While they were there, God gave Moses the Law. It told them how they were to live to please God. God was showing them more of Himself all the time. He wanted them to learn how to depend upon Him for every need of their lives. He gave them food and water in the desert and protected them from their enemies.

LEVITICUS

Leviticus was very important to the Hebrews because it gave many laws about the work of the priests. These men were chosen by God and set apart for His work. This means that they didn't have any other job except God's work. The people thought of them as being holy men. They were to speak to the people for God and show them His ways. Leviticus also gave many rules about how the people were to keep healthy, handle quarrels, and worship.

WORDS TO KNOW   miracles (MIR uh kuhlz) — *things only God can do.*

Jewish high priest

Today, we don't need to do *all* the laws listed in this book, because Jesus has come. The Bible says that He was our High Priest. He was also the Lamb of God, the only sacrifice we need. Our sins are forgiven by believing this sacrifice was for us and accepting Jesus Christ as our own personal Savior. However, in this book, we can learn a great deal about what is pleasing to God.

NUMBERS

This book is called Numbers because it tells about two times when the people were "numbered," or counted. It tells us more of the story about the Israelites in the **wilderness**. They lived in tents in this desert region for over 40 years. During these years, God was still trying to teach them about Himself. He wanted them to believe in Him with all their hearts. He renewed the covenant . At last, the people came to the border of the Promised Land.

DEUTERONOMY

Deuteronomy repeats much of the Law. Some of it sounds just like the scriptures in

---

WORDS TO KNOW wilderness (WIL der nis)— *a wild forest or desert place.*

Exodus. This is because Deuteronomy gives the speeches Moses made to the people just before he died. They were about to go into Canaan, the Promised Land. This land had been promised as part of the covenant to Moses and his family hundreds of years earlier. Moses reminded them of the greatness of God's love for them. Then he warned them to keep their part of the covenant so that God could bless them. You will want to know what this Law was all about. The Ten Commandments are found in Exodus 20 and in Deuteronomy 5. Find those places and read them for yourself. You may even want to memorize them.

OLD TESTAMENT HISTORY

The next 12 books in the Bible are books of history. They're divided into three groups according to the history they tell about. Joshua, Judges, and Ruth are about the period of *Theocracy* (thē O kra sē). The three double books of Samuel, Kings, and Chronicles are about the *Monarchy* (MON ar kē). The last three, Ezra, Nehemiah, and Esther are called *Post Exile* (EG zīl) books. As we walk through these books, see if you can picture in your mind what was happening. It covers many years, but it all leads up to the coming of Jesus Christ. Therefore, it's helpful to the Bible student to know at least a little of this story of the Hebrews.

THEOCRACY

The first three books of history give the story of the Hebrews during the time that God was their only King. He would speak to the priests, and they would tell the people what God had said. When the people needed something from God, they

18

would go to the priest. The priest would prepare a sacrifice and talk to God about the problem. This period of Hebrew history is called the Theocracy. It means "ruled by God."

The Israelites were a theocracy for many years. Then they grew tired of serving a God they couldn't see. They saw their Canaanite friends worshiping gods made out of wood or stone or even gold or silver. The Canaanites were the people who lived in the land when the Israelites came. Most of them had been killed or driven out, but some were allowed to live among the Hebrews. This tempted the Hebrews to do just what they had promised God they would *not* do. They bowed down and worshiped idols. God could no longer bless them with His protection. When an enemy nation came to attack them, God couldn't help them.

Sacrifice burning on an altar

JOSHUA

Joshua is named for the man who became leader of the Hebrews after Moses died. It tells how Joshua led the whole nation into the Promised Land. He prayed, and God told him how to conquer the people who were living there.

You'll enjoy the exciting stories in this book. God did some great miracles for His people. He made the water of the Jordan River stop flowing so the people could cross on dry land. Then he told them how

to bring down the walls of the city of Jericho by just marching around the city.

JUDGES

Judges describes events which happened after the land was conquered and settled. The people gradually quit worshiping the true God. They began to bow down to the idols of the Canaanites. By doing this, they broke their covenant with God. When other countries came into their land and fought them, the Hebrews had no power. They had to surrender to their enemies. While they were being ruled by the enemy nation, they suffered greatly.

Sometimes they became slaves. Sometimes they had to pay high taxes that left them very little for themselves. After a number of years of this, the people would repent and cry out to God. He would hear their prayers and send a leader to help them fight and get their freedom back. The leader was called a *judge*. This situation went on for many generations, and there were many **judges** during this time. That's why this book is given this name.

A LAMP UNTO MY FEET

Study to show thyself approved unto God, a workman that needeth not to be ashamed, rightly dividing the word of truth. (II Timothy 2:15)

WORDS TO KNOW

judges (JUJ ez) — *leaders chosen by God to deliver His people from foreign oppressors.*

RUTH

Ruth is a story about a young woman from a foreign country who came to live with her mother-in-law in Canaan during the period of the Judges. That's why her story is placed in this group. Everyone enjoys reading the story of Ruth. It's a story about love. It shows the love that Ruth had for her mother-in-law Naomi. They had both become widows in the land of Moab. When they returned to Israel, they were very poor. Naomi sent Ruth to gather wheat in the field of a rich man named Boaz. Later, this man became her husband. Their great-grandson was King David, and it was from the line of David that Jesus came.

MONARCHY

After many generations of being led by Judges, the people began to ask for a king. They wanted to be like all the other nations. Of course, God knew it was better for them to serve Him only. At last, however, He let them have a king. There were three kings during this period — Saul, David, and Solomon. Sometimes it's called the period of the United Kingdom.

When Solomon died, some of the people didn't want to be ruled by his son. They chose another king and started a separate nation. It was called Israel, or the Northern Kingdom. The people of Judah, the Southern Kingdom, chose to follow Solomon's son, and they had their own country. This period of Hebrew history is called the period of the Divided Kingdom.

I SAMUEL   II SAMUEL

I Samuel takes up the nation's history with the last of the Judges. His name was Samuel. The story about his birth and childhood is a good one. You'll want to read it. It was about this time that the people began to ask for a king. Samuel was led by God to find a man named Saul.

Samuel **anointed** Saul with oil and announced that Saul was now king of the Hebrew nation. Saul was a very good king

City of David

WORDS TO KNOW

anointed (uh NOINT ed) — set apart for God; usually in a ceremony in which oil was poured on the head of the person being anointed.

20

at first, but he wasn't obedient to God during the last part of his life. During this time, Samuel continued to be the spiritual leader of the people. Finally, God sent him to anoint David to be the king. This book tells about David killing Goliath and about his experiences as a musician in the court of Saul. It tells about his friendship with Saul's son, Jonathan, and about his narrow escapes from Saul's attempts to kill him.

II Samuel is a history of the reign of David. He was a warrior and, with God's help, conquered all the enemies that had oppressed Israel for many generations. It was David who decided to make Jerusalem the capital of the country. During David's reign, it became a beautiful city.

David loved God very much and was skillful in praising Him. Most of the Psalms were made up by David as he sang and played on his harp. Perhaps that is why God loved David so much.

There were many difficult times for David during his time as king. He even had a son who tried to take away his kingdom. But he always turned to God for help. And when he did wrong, he would confess his sin and ask God to forgive him.

I KINGS	II KINGS

I and II Kings are in two books because they're long. I Kings tells how the nation became rich and powerful under the reign of David's son, Solomon. It was the greatest time in all of Hebrew history. People came from far countries to see the splendid Temple these Hebrews had built in Jerusalem.

The rest of I Kings and II Kings tells how the nation became divided. The reigns of the kings of both countries are described. The writer then tells whether the king obeyed God's laws or if he led the people of his kingdom to worship idols.

Sometimes the people of the two kingdoms were friendly with each other, but much of the time they were enemies. The two books follow Israel and Judah

from the reign of Solomon until the Exile. When we read these books, we get to know more about God and how He deals with people.

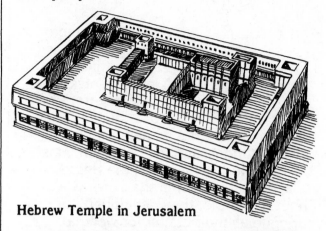

Hebrew Temple in Jerusalem

I CHRONICLES	II CHRONICLES

I and II Chronicles give us almost exactly the same record that we find in II Samuel and I and II Kings. However, the writer of these two books was not just interested in what happened. He gives us much more about the spiritual importance of the events. These books show us that God will judge men and nations according to their obedience of His Law.

POST EXILE

The last three books of history are called Post Exile books. While the people of Judah were obedient to God, He would bless them. Finally, they turned away from Him so much that it was necessary to punish them. He allowed both kingdoms to be captured by powerful enemy nations. Israel was first. Her people became slaves of the cruel Assyrians (uh SI rē unz). These people took the families of Israel away from their homeland and scattered them throughout the Assyrian Empire.

Later, Judah was conquered by the Babylonians (bab i LŌ nē unz). All her strongest people were taken as slaves to Babylonia, far to the east. Only a few old, weak people were left in the homeland. Beautiful Jerusalem lay in **ruins**. The Temple was completely destroyed.

The people of Judah lived many years in

Israelite captives

this faraway land of Babylonia. Their captors called them "Jews," a nickname that came from the word "Judah." The Babylonians were not as harsh with their captives as the Assyrians had been. Most of the time during the exile, the Hebrews were allowed to worship their own God. Without a Temple, they developed the synagogue as their center for worship. They remained faithful to God throughout the years of captivity, but they were often sad for the sins that had led them into this trouble. They took their harps with them, but they refused to play them. As a symbol of their sadness, they hung their harps on the trees until the day they could be free.

Eventually, Babylonia was conquered by a more powerful nation, Persia. The Persian king, Cyrus, was more helpful to the Hebrews than the Babylonian kings had been. He gave permission for a group of them to return to their land to rebuild the city of Jerusalem. Three of the books of history tell about this return and the events in the years which followed. That's why they are call Post Exile books. The word *post* means "after."

EZRA

Ezra is one of the Post Exile books. It tells about the first group of exiles who returned to Jerusalem. It shows the great trouble they had trying to rebuild among the ruins of Jerusalem. Ezra was a priest and <u>scribe</u> who returned with the second

WORDS TO KNOW

ruins (ROO inz) — *the remains of a fallen building or city.*
scribe (skrīb) — *a person who writes for another person.*

group of exiles about 57 years after the first. He found the first settlers discouraged about their work. They had even fallen away from the keeping of the Law. He worked to encourage them and to lead them back to the worship of God.

NEHEMIAH

The book of Nehemiah was written about the same historical period as the book of Ezra. Nehemiah's story begins with the King of Persia granting him permission to return to Jerusalem. Nehemiah was appointed governor and was sent to help with the rebuilding of the wall around the city. Because there were enemies trying to stop them, the people were forced to work very hard and fast. They were prepared to stop and fight at any time. When the wall was finally completed, there was great rejoicing. Later, Nehemiah returned to the Persian court. He had been in Jerusalem about 12 years.

ESTHER

Esther is a story about a young Hebrew girl who became queen of Persia. Persia is the country that overtook Babylonia while the Jews were still in captivity there. Esther was one of those who did *not* return

to Jerusalem after the exile. She remained faithful to the worship of God, however. When she found out about a cruel plot to kill all the Jews in the entire kingdom, Esther risked her life to go before the king and ask him to save her people. It was such an important event in Hebrew history that the Jews still celebrate the victory every year.

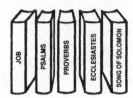

POETRY

Among all nations, there are a few people who have a special ability to share their deep feelings and thoughts through poetry and beautiful words of wisdom. The next five books of the Bible include some of these writings of the Hebrew people. Sometimes these books are called Books of Literature instead of Books of Poetry. Job, Proverbs, and Ecclesiastes are known as "Wisdom Literature." Psalms and the Song of Solomon are really songs. Some of the Psalms were actually used by the Hebrews in their worship. Many verses from the Psalms have been put to music and are sung in churches today. The book of Lamentations is sometimes listed as a poetry book.

A LAMP UNTO MY FEET

Thy word have I hid in mine heart, that I might not sin against thee. (Psalm 119:11)

JOB

Job is the story of a man who loved God and always lived a righteous life. God let Satan test Job by causing him to lose his family, his riches, and his health. Some of Job's friends came to comfort him. They tried to explain why he was having so much trouble. Their words and Job's answers are all written as poetry. Job remained faithful to God during all his time of suffering. God blessed him by restoring his wealth, giving him more children, and letting him live a long and healthy life.

PSALMS

The Psalms are a collection of 150 poems and hymns. Most were written by David, but some were by other writers. They tell about the greatness and faithfulness of God. Many of them were sung in the Temple as part of the worship.

The Psalms are, perhaps, the most read and quoted and loved of all scriptures in the Bible. They help us worship God. Most of us find that they say just what we feel ourselves. Many people have a favorite Psalm. Some are very good for memorizing.

PROVERBS

Proverbs is also a much-quoted book. It's really a collection of wise sayings. Much of it came from Solomon, one of the wisest men who ever lived. Proverbs gives much helpful advice for living a successful life. Its value never grows out of date. It's still quite useful to anyone who will read it and obey it. Many Proverbs are good memory verses.

ECCLESIASTES

Ecclesiastes is another of the books of wisdom literature. No one can be certain who wrote it. The author, whoever he was, wanted to find the best purpose for living. He tried many different things — wealth, fame, wisdom, and pleasure. Eventually, the author decided that man is just supposed to enjoy all of the good things God has given him and that he must obey God's commandments if he wants to find true and lasting happiness.

SONG OF SOLOMON

The Song of Solomon is a love song. It tells a story about a young girl who was taken to the court of a king. No one knows exactly why it is called by the name "Solomon." It might have been about the court of King Solomon. The king loved the girl for her great beauty, but she was still in love with a shepherd somewhere else. The song tells of their love for each other.

Some people think this story may have been put into the Bible because it shows how much God loves His people and how they should love Him even though they are offered great wealth by other "gods."

MAJOR PROPHETS

Prophets played a very important part in the history of the Hebrews. These men were usually dedicated to God and spent much time in study and prayer. This helped them to be prepared to speak God's messages to the people. Often these messages were given as speeches. Sometimes they were written down by the prophet himself, or by one of his students, or a scribe.

There are 17 books of prophecy in our Old Testament. The first five are called Major Prophets. This isn't because they are more important than the others. It's just because they are longer books and include more teaching than the Minor Prophets. Each book is named for the man who wrote it except for Lamentations, which was Jeremiah's second book.

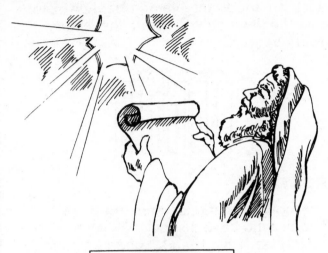

ISAIAH

Isaiah is about a prophet of Judah, the Southern Kingdom. He had a strong influence on the events of his day. He lived through the reigns of four kings. During this time, his small country was threatened by the powerful armies of Assyria and Egypt. God used Isaiah to declare His greatness and holiness to the people. Through Isaiah, God warned the Hebrews to be faithful and __devoted__ to Him and to turn away from all other gods. Isaiah was given God's words to predict the coming of the Messiah. That word means "anointed one," and it always refers to Jesus Christ. He was anointed to redeem all people to God who would believe in Him.

JEREMIAH

Jeremiah lived and prophesied in Judah many years after Isaiah. He was prophesying during the 40 years before the capture of Jerusalem, when the people became sinful and stubborn. They were

WORDS TO KNOW   devoted (di VO tid) — *set apart for God to serve Him only.*

listening to false prophets, men who told them untrue things and pretended that God had said it. The false prophets were really trying to please the people. But Jeremiah was inspired by God. He could see that God wasn't interested in the people's sacrifices if they didn't really love Him. He wanted His laws down in their hearts. All of Jeremiah's prophecies were from God, but the people didn't want to hear them. This made Jeremiah very unpopular, but he kept right on telling them what God told him to say.

LAMENTATIONS

Lamentations is grouped with the Books of Prophecy because Bible scholars believe it is another part of the writings of Jeremiah. It's actually a collection of poems. The word lamentation means "deep sorrow." The prophet is lamenting, or sorrowing, over the destruction of Jerusalem which he knew was about to take place. Because of this, Jeremiah is sometimes called "the weeping prophet."

EZEKIEL

Ezekiel was a prophet and priest who lived among the Jews and preached to them during their exile in Babylonia. He spoke to the people in many strange pictures and symbols, trying to get them to seek God. He wanted them to do God's will and to have faith in their future. Ezekiel's

visions were given to Him by God. He foretold many things that are to happen before the end of time. Therefore, they are important for us today, too. Many Bible scholars spend much time studying Ezekiel.

DANIEL

Daniel, also, was a Jewish captive. When he arrived in Babylonia, the king took him into his own court. God gave Daniel a special gift for interpreting dreams. Daniel was able to explain the dream of one king and this saved many lives. Once, wicked men made a plan to get Daniel killed, but God saved him from the lions that were supposed to eat him.

Daniel told about visions he had which are difficult for us to understand. He prophesied about the Day of Judgment, or the time of the end. Bible students today can learn much from reading Daniel.

MINOR PROPHETS

The next 12 books in the Bible are called the Minor Prophets because they're very brief compared to the books of the Major Prophets. And yet, some of them have given us valuable information and important prophecies. As you become a better Bible student, you'll want to read these books.

HOSEA

Hosea was one of only two prophets whose messages were for the people of Israel, the Northern Kingdom. Hosea had an unfaithful wife. He thought the covenant between God and His people was like the pledge between a husband and wife. Even though we may break the covenant and go away from our God, He still loves us. God forgives us and even buys us back from slavery to sin just as Hosea forgave his wife and bought her back from slavery.

JOEL

Joel warns about a terrible time when locusts would invade the land, leaving the country almost destroyed. He was preaching to Judah. It isn't clear whether Joel was predicting a real invasion of insects or describing an invasion by an enemy nation. He predicted the Day of the Lord will be even more terrible than what he was describing. He called people to repent and pray and put their hope in God.

AMOS

Amos came from his home in Judah to preach to the people of the Northern Kingdom. He lived at a time when Israel had a large army and was enjoying prosperity. But the rich people had become evil and were often drunk. Some of them made life very hard for the poor people. Their worship was only outward and wasn't from their hearts. Amos warned them that this would lead to punishment unless they repented and turned to God. He said they were to show their love for God by the way they treated one another.

OBADIAH

Obadiah isn't divided into chapters because it has only 21 verses. The prophet was actually predicting the future of another country named Edom. Edom had been a bitter enemy of Judah for many generations. When Judah was captured, Edom mocked the people and even helped destroy the beautiful city of Jerusalem. Obadiah foretold that Edom, herself, would be destroyed someday, but God's people would return and become even greater than ever.

JONAH

The book of Jonah is a story about a man named Jonah, but it probably wasn't written by him. God told Jonah to take a message to the wicked city of Nineveh in Assyria. Because this country had been a cruel enemy of the Hebrews for a long time, Jonah didn't want to go. He tried to run far away so he wouldn't have to do what God said. The story tells about his adventures with a great fish, with the wicked city, and with a vine. It shows us how very much God loves and wants to save everyone.

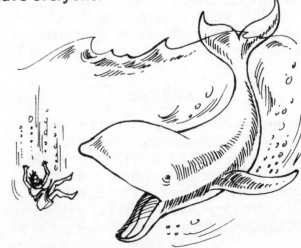

26

MICAH

Micah lived during the time of Isaiah. He predicted the destruction of Jerusalem and Samaria, the capital of the Northern Kingdom. He also predicted the coming of the Messiah. He said this Messiah would be born in Bethlehem and would eventually become king over all people. Micah was upset by the way people treated one another. He said that God is interested in a true religion of <u>justice</u> and righteousness.

NAHUM

Nahum wrote many years after the events described in the book of Jonah. He wrote about the city of Nineveh, too. By this time, however, Nineveh was a very large city with high, strong walls. It had become so sinful that it was beyond forgiving. Therefore, Nahum predicted that it would be completely destroyed for its wickedness.

HABAKKUK

Habakkuk was a prophet in Judah soon after Nahum. He was also upset by the wickedness of the people. He was even angrier when he learned God was sending the hated Chaldeans (kal DE unz) to be the ones to punish them. Chaldeans is another name for Babylonians. God made sure that Habakkuk understood that the evil Chaldeans would be punished, too. God's message through Habakkuk is that His righteous ones are to keep faithful to Him and He will bless them.

ZEPHANIAH

Zephaniah prophesied to Judah before the exile. He believed that men were so evil God would have to judge them. He prophesied about a "Day of the Lord" which would come to Judah. On that terrible day, the unrighteous would be wiped out, but the few righteous ones would be saved.

HAGGAI

Haggai was a prophet of the post exile period. Judah finally fell to the Babylonians. The people were taken as slaves to Babylonia. After 70 years, a large group of them returned to Jerusalem to rebuild the city and the temple. Haggai was one of them. When the people became discouraged and stopped the building of the temple, Haggai came and preached to them. He helped them to remember to put God's work first. Then they could trust God to help them with their own needs.

ZECHARIAH

Zechariah was a young man who preached at about the same time as Haggai. He told the people of Jerusalem to repent of their sins and to finish the temple. He made many predictions about the coming Messiah. His writings describe eight visions about the final victory of God's people on the earth.

MALACHI

Malachi saw that life was hard for God's people in Jerusalem, even after the temple

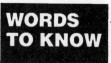

WORDS TO KNOW

justice (JUS tis) — *fair reward or punishment for something a person has done.*

was rebuilt. Sinful people seemed to be doing well. Many of those who tried to be righteous had become discouraged and stopped giving God their best. Their hearts were no longer in their worship. The priests themselves were leading the people into sin. Malachi told the people that they should keep their faith in God and keep putting Him first. He assured them there would be a day when all nations and all men would have to be judged and would have to pay for their evil deeds.

A LAMP UNTO MY FEET

The grass withereth, the flower fadeth: but the word of our God shall stand forever. (Isaiah 40:8)

BETWEEN THE OLD AND NEW TESTAMENTS

The prophecy of the Old Testament ended with Malachi. Four hundred years went by before another prophet came to tell about the coming Messiah. That prophet was John the Baptist. During those four centuries, the Hebrews were conquered and ruled by several different countries. The Persian Empire remained in power for many years with one strong king after another.

In Europe, meanwhile, another strong nation was growing in power. Philip of Macedon (MAS i don) conquered and united the Greeks. Then, his famous son, Alexander the Great, led his Greek army to conquer the great Persian empire. Of course, this included Palestine. The Hebrews now submitted to Greek control for many years.

Farther to the west, another great power was growing. The Romans, led by emperors greedy to rule the world, marched through one country after another. Palestine, of course, was one of those countries that came under Roman rule.

Ruled by force   Rules by love

All the time, there were faithful people who kept the Law of Moses. They remembered God's covenant with His chosen people, and they cried out for the Messiah to come and deliver them from their persecution and hardship. Finally, the Messiah was born into this troubled Roman world. He would prove to be the most powerful of all rulers — the King of Kings. His kingdom would be in the hearts of those who would believe Him, and He would not rule with fear. He would rule with love.

THE NEW TESTAMENT

The Old Testament story prepared the way for the coming of the Messiah. The New Testament is the story of His birth, His life and teachings, His death and **resurrection**. Then, it tells what happened after Jesus went back to heaven. We learn of the events of the early Church and the

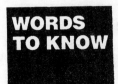 **WORDS TO KNOW** resurrection (REZ uh REK shun) — *coming to life again after having been dead; raised from the dead.*

28

men and women who gave their lives to the spread of this Gospel message.

There are four kinds of writings in the New Testament:

- The four Gospels tell the life and teachings of Jesus.
- The Acts of the Apostles is the only book of history. It tells about the beginning of the Church.
- Twenty-one of the books are epistles. This is another word for "letters." Paul wrote thirteen of them, and eight were written by other apostles. In our study, we will consider these as two separate divisions.
- The only book of prophecy is The Revelation. It tells about the events that will take place just before the second coming of Jesus.

GOSPELS

Each of the four Gospel writers had a different purpose for writing his story of the life and teachings of Jesus. Mark probably wrote his first. Matthew and Luke may have used some of his information in their stories. And yet, each man added something from his own memory. Each was inspired by the Holy Spirit to write what God wanted him to say. Read these books over and over. It's a very good way to get to know the Son of God.

A LAMP UNTO MY FEET

Think not that I am come to destroy the law, or the prophets: I am not come to destroy, but to fulfill.
(Matthew 5:17)

MATTHEW

Matthew was one of the men chosen by Jesus to be His disciples. This means they stayed with Jesus most of the time while Jesus was preaching and teaching and healing. He was showing the men He chose how they were to minister to people when He would no longer be here on earth in person.

Matthew wanted to tell the Jews about Jesus. He wanted them to see that this man was truly the Messiah predicted by the prophets. Matthew keeps quoting and referring to the Old Testament Scriptures. His book is sometimes known as the Gospel of the Kingdom. Matthew tells about the Wise Men who came to find the one who was born King of the Jews. They had read the Old Testament prophecies and knew from the star that He had come.

The teachings of Jesus in the Gospels often deal with the Kingdom of God. As we read Matthew's story, we cannot help but see our Lord as the promised King. It should help us to want Him to be King of our lives, too.

MARK

Mark wasn't one of the original 12 disciples. He was probably a very young man at the time Jesus was ministering.

Mark's mother was a Christian, and his Uncle Barnabas was one of the first missionaries. Mark even went along on the first missionary trip. He later became an **evangelist** himself and worked with the new churches.

As you know, the world of that day was under Roman rule. Mark knew that the Romans would not be at all interested in seeing Jesus as the One who fulfilled Old Testament prophecy. He wanted to write so that Roman people could be saved. Therefore, he showed them Jesus as a man of divine power. His story is full of action.

LUKE

Luke wasn't one of the twelve disciples, either. In fact, he was the only Scripture writer who wasn't even a Jew. He was Greek. Luke had been educated to be a doctor and was quite interested in the healing miracles of Jesus. That's why you can read about many of these in Luke's Gospel.

WORDS TO KNOW evangelist (i VAN juh list)— *a traveling preacher of the Gospel.*

Dr. Luke was with Paul on some of his missionary trips. Paul probably found him quite useful in the work of the churches.

Since Luke was a Greek Gentile, he wrote his story to help other Greek Gentiles who had become Christians. A Gentile was any person who wasn't a Jew. Luke wanted to show them Jesus as the Divine Son of Man who came to save all mankind — not just the Jews.

JOHN

John was one of the three disciples mentioned most in the Gospel stories. He loved Jesus very much and tried to stay as close to Him as possible. Jesus loved John, too. John is often referred to as the "beloved disciple."

After Jesus went back to heaven, John became a strong preacher of the Gospel. For a long time he was exiled to the island of Patmos. The Romans sent him there to punish him for preaching about Jesus. Later, he was allowed to return to Ephesus, where he lived to be an old man.

By this time, the other Gospels had been written and copied many times. Paul and Peter had been killed, and all the other disciples had died. John must have known that he would die soon also. The Holy Spirit inspired him to write this Gospel story. He tells us why he wrote it in John 20:31.

But these are written, that ye might believe that Jesus is the Christ, the Son of God; and that believing ye might have life through his name. (John 20:31)

John wrote his Gospel story to meet the spiritual needs of the Church. He knew Christians would continue to face great persecution in the days ahead. He wanted to show them that Jesus Christ was truly the Divine Son of God. John's Gospel includes more of the teachings of Jesus than any other writer.

NEW TESTAMENT HISTORY

THE ACTS

The Gospels tell us about Jesus Christ who came to show us the Father. This book, the Acts of the Apostles, tells us about the Holy Spirit, who was sent by the Father to show us Christ. It's the only book of history in the New Testament.

It begins with Jesus telling His followers not to start preaching until they had been given power from on high. When the Holy Spirit came, the power came. This is still true today. The Holy Spirit gives Christians boldness to witness to others about Jesus. As a Teacher, the Holy Spirit helps us understand what the Bible is saying to us personally.

The author of the book of Acts is the same Dr. Luke who wrote the Gospel account of the life of Christ. Luke meant for this book to be a continuation of his first book. Therefore, he gives us the history of the early days of the Church and the efforts of the new Christians to spread the Gospel message. Much of it is about the work of the Apostle Paul and his helpers. These missionaries took the Good News about Jesus to many of the countries around the Mediterranean Sea. By the end of Acts, we see the Church growing strong all through the Roman Empire.

A LAMP UNTO MY FEET

Heaven and earth shall pass away: but my words shall not pass away. (Mark 13:31)

PAUL'S EPISTLES

The next 21 books of the New Testament are the epistles (letters). The first 13 were written by Paul — nine of them to churches and the other four to individuals. Paul was a well-trained leader among the Jews in Jerusalem. He heard what the Christians were preaching, and he was working hard to stop it. But Jesus appeared to him in a vision. He told Paul that He was going to send him to preach the Gospel to the Gentiles. From that day, Paul gave himself to the Lord. He spent all of his life trying to get others to know Jesus and to live for Him.

Paul started churches in Asia Minor and Greece. Even while he was prisoner in Rome, he kept telling the story of Jesus. The letters he wrote are very helpful to us today. We can learn much about Jesus from what Paul wrote to others.

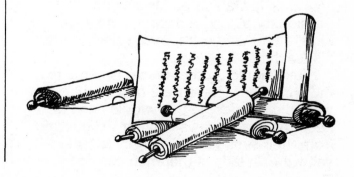

ROMANS

In the church at Rome, there were both Jews and Gentiles. Paul wrote this letter to encourage them. Paul wanted them to understand what Jesus had done for them when He died on the cross. His death paid for the sins of every person in the whole world. When the sinner accepts this by faith, then his sin is forgiven. God sees him just as if he had never sinned. Paul had been a sinner before Jesus appeared to him, but now he knew that he was different. All the bad things he had done to the Christians had been forgiven. Isn't it wonderful to know that this forgiveness is for us, too?

I CORINTHIANS   II CORINTHIANS

Paul wrote two letters to the church in Corinth, a city in Greece. Christians there were having some problems in the church and had written to Paul asking what they should do. When his first letter cheered and comforted the people, Paul wrote a second letter. They needed more instruction. He wanted them to see how to apply love to their own problems and their church problems.

In the Church today, we still have many of the same problems the Corinthian church had. When we read Paul's letters, we know we're reading what God wants us to do. His lessons on love are valuable reminders for us, too.

GALATIANS

Galatia (guh LĀ shuh) was a district in Asia Minor. Paul stopped to visit the churches in Galatia on his second missionary trip. The people there were kind to Paul and were always glad to hear his teachings.

After Paul left, other teachers came to the churches. These were false teachers who told the people they would need to keep the Jewish laws in order to be saved from their sins. Paul wrote this letter to show the Galatians that man can do

nothing to earn his salvation because it's a free gift from God. Jesus Christ is all we need.

EPHESIANS

Ephesus (EH fi sus) was a large city in Asia Minor. The people who lived there worshiped idols. They had built a big, beautiful temple to their favorite goddess, Diana. When Paul went to Ephesus, he found some Jews and immediately went to their meeting and preached to them about Jesus. Soon he had a church started. It grew to be a very strong church.

Paul wrote this letter to the Ephesians to help them see how all things are brought together in Christ. He taught them that the Church is the Body of Christ and that everyone who loves Christ and has been saved belongs to His Body. Paul said Christians must learn to work together just the way a person's body works. Each part must do its job, or the body can't work properly.

PHILIPPIANS

Philippi (FIL i pī) was the first city in Europe where the Gospel message was preached. Paul wrote this letter from his prison cell in Rome where he was awaiting his trial. Other Christians were being put to death for their beliefs and Paul knew that he could die any time. Yet, his letter is full of his own joy in Christ. He urges the

Church to rejoice in this wonderful Lord, too.

Christians today need this message of joy. There are times when it isn't easy to be a Christian. Reading this letter from Paul will help us keep our joy.

COLOSSIANS

The city of Colossae (kuh LOS ī) was in Asia Minor, about 100 miles east of Ephesus. In this letter, Paul wanted to remind the Christians to be careful about what they were hearing. False teachers were coming into the Church telling the people that they had to do certain things to earn their salvation. Christ has delivered us from the power of darkness and taken us into the kingdom of God. It's a free gift.

This letter includes many helpful teachings for the Christian who wants to "walk worthy of the Lord" and "increase in the knowledge of God."

I THESSALONIANS

II THESSALONIANS

These two letters were written by Paul to the church in the Greek city of Thessalonica (THES ah lō NĪ kah). The people there had asked some questions about Paul's <u>authority</u>. His first letter was to answer these doubts and to encourage the Church, which was suffering persecution. He does this by telling them about the second coming of Christ, the time when our Lord will return to earth again and take all those who have believed in Him to be with Him forever in His Kingdom. The second letter strengthens what was taught in the first one.

I TIMOTHY   II TIMOTHY
TITUS

The two letters to Timothy and the letter to Titus are called <u>pastoral</u> epistles. Timothy and Titus were young preachers. Paul gave them advice about their personal lives and about their work with the churches. From these letters we can learn about the way the early Church was organized.

In I Timothy, Paul lists the <u>qualifications</u> of church officers. By that time, the churches were growing and needed some local people to be leaders. Deacons were chosen to look after the physical needs of the local church and its members. Elders and bishops were selected to be the spiritual leaders. It was important to have the right kind of men in these positions. Churches today often have these same officers.

In II Timothy, Paul deals with the personal life and character of a Christian. He tells us how to keep ourselves pure and holy.

Titus also lists the qualifications for elders and bishops. This letter also has

WORDS TO KNOW
authority (uh THŌR i tē) — *the power or right to lead other people.*

WORDS TO KNOW
pastoral (PAS tu rul) — *having to do with the pastor of a church.*
qualifications (KWOL uh fuh CĀ shunz) — *that which makes a person fit for a job, task, or office.*

good advice about how to live as a Christian.

Can you see how these books can help a good Bible student today? We still have officers in churches. It helps to know what kind of people to choose. And anyone who loves Jesus and wants to live for Him will want to know Paul's advice to Timothy.

PHILEMON

Philemon is more like a personal note than an epistle. It's written to a man named Philemon and to the church that met in his house. Paul sent the letter to ask Philemon to take back his runaway slave, Onesimus (ō NES i mus). He wanted Philemon to forgive Onesimus and to help him.

A LAMP UNTO MY FEET

All scripture is given by inspiration of God, and is profitable for doctrine, for reproof, for correction, for instruction in righteousness; That the man of God may be perfect, thoroughly furnished unto all good works. (II Timothy 3:16-17)

GENERAL EPISTLES

The last eight epistles are called "general" because they were not written to certain people or churches. They were for Christians everywhere. Paul's letters and the book of Hebrews were named for the people who received them. The last seven epistles were given the names of the men who wrote them.

HEBREWS

No one knows who wrote the book of Hebrews or when he wrote it. Some Bible scholars think Paul was the author, and they list it with his other letters. That could be true, but there's no proof. We do know it was addressed to Hebrew Christians. The Jews believed in Jesus, but it was very difficult for them to let go of their Jewish traditions. The writer of Hebrews wanted to show them that Christ was greater than all the prophets and priests and teachers of all time. Christ gave Himself as the only sacrifice we would ever need, and He brought in a better covenant, which we are under now. When we believe that Jesus' blood paid for our sins, then we enter into the covenant with God, too. It means that, in the eyes of God, we are the same as Jesus.

JAMES

There were three disciples named James. The one who wrote this epistle was probably the brother of Jesus. He was the leader of the church at Jerusalem for many years. Eventually, he was killed by some of the Jews who were trying to stop the Word from being preached.

In this letter James tells all Christians that their faith in Jesus should be seen in their daily living. James tells us about controlling our tongue and our attitudes.

I PETER   II PETER

Peter was one of the 12 original disciples. He wrote his letters during the time when Christians were suffering greatly under the cruel laws of the Romans. Peter may have been in danger himself, or he may even have been in prison when he wrote.

Peter's first letter is filled with hope for the persecuted Christians. He taught that our hope must be based upon trust in God and that we must love Him more than we love life.

In II Peter, he warns against false teachers who will come and try to lead Christians away from the truth of God's Word. He also gives assurance that Christ will come again to bring a new heaven and a new earth.

I JOHN   II JOHN
III JOHN

These three letters were written by the same man who wrote the Gospel of John. He wrote them to strengthen the faith of believers.

Some of the Christians had the idea that it doesn't matter what a person believes as long as he's sincere. In his first letter, we see that John was trying to get Christians to see that what we believe will determine

how we live. Therefore, what we believe is very important. John assures Christians that Jesus was both human and divine. God was revealed to us in the man called Jesus. John also deals with the need to love one another more.

In his second letter, John warns against false teachers and again reminds us of the need for Christian love.

In III John, he encourages Christians to help with the spread of the Gospel message.

JUDE

Jude wasn't one of the disciples. He may, however have been a brother of Jesus. No one knows when or where the letter was written. Jude warned Christians against the false teachers who were disturbing the Church. He called the Church back to the teachings of the apostles.

REVELATION

A PROPHETIC BOOK

REVELATION

Revelation is different from all the other books in the Bible. It was written by John, the Gospel writer. John was an exile on the island of Patmos at the time. He describes a vision in which he saw events that would take place at the end of history.

This writing is filled with symbols. There are numbers and scrolls and seals and beasts and many angels. It isn't easy to know the meanings of these symbols. And yet, it was very important to the Christians in the churches that first heard them. In his book, John wanted to reassure the Church that Christ would come again and would conquer every enemy.

More people are reading Revelation today than ever before. Perhaps it's because the events described in the book seem to be coming to pass in our own time. Bible students who know this book can hear the news each day with more understanding.

As the events of Revelation take place, we're to keep praising God more and more and to live each day for Jesus. But most of all, we're to keep telling others about this wonderful Jesus who came to give us eternal life.

TIME LINE OF HUMAN HISTORY

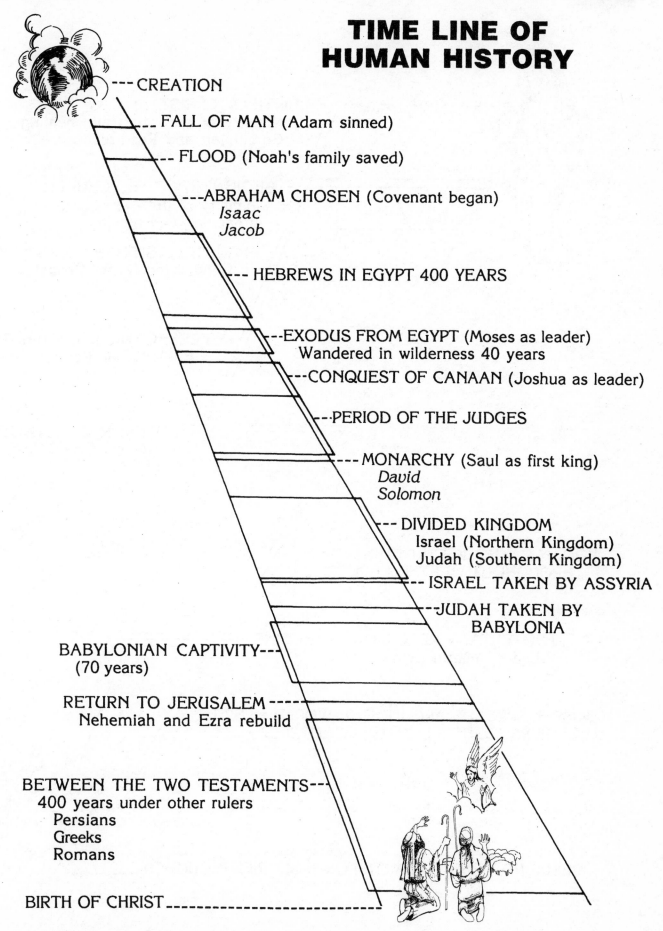

--- CREATION

--- FALL OF MAN (Adam sinned)

--- FLOOD (Noah's family saved)

---ABRAHAM CHOSEN (Covenant began)
  Isaac
  Jacob

--- HEBREWS IN EGYPT 400 YEARS

---EXODUS FROM EGYPT (Moses as leader)
Wandered in wilderness 40 years

---CONQUEST OF CANAAN (Joshua as leader)

--PERIOD OF THE JUDGES

----MONARCHY (Saul as first king)
  David
  Solomon

--- DIVIDED KINGDOM
Israel (Northern Kingdom)
Judah (Southern Kingdom)

-- ISRAEL TAKEN BY ASSYRIA

--JUDAH TAKEN BY
        BABYLONIA

BABYLONIAN CAPTIVITY---
(70 years)

RETURN TO JERUSALEM ----
Nehemiah and Ezra rebuild

BETWEEN THE TWO TESTAMENTS---
400 years under other rulers
Persians
Greeks
Romans

BIRTH OF CHRIST

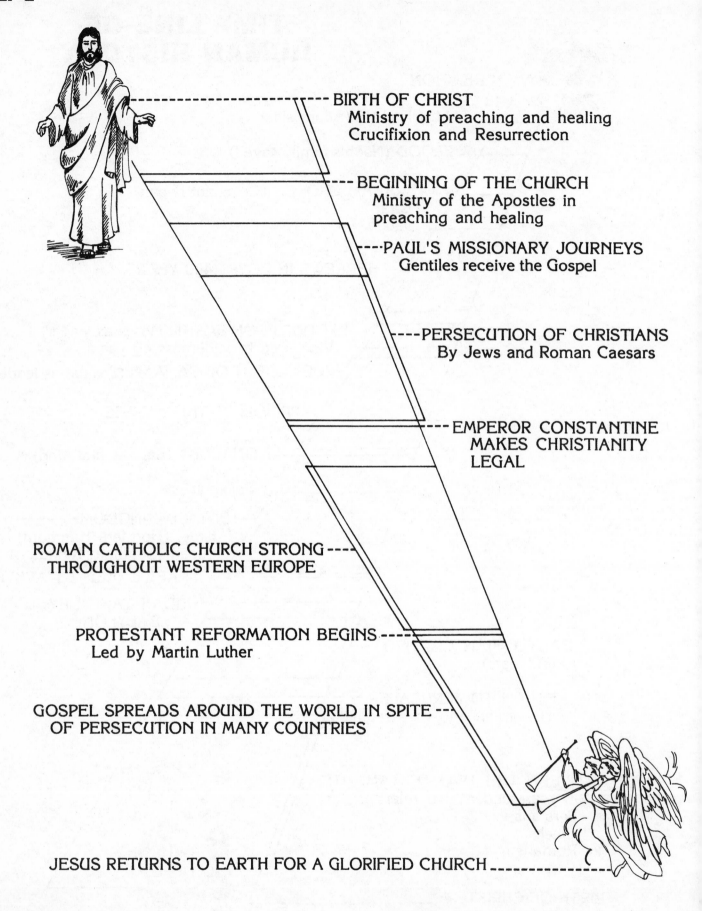

BIRTH OF CHRIST
Ministry of preaching and healing
Crucifixion and Resurrection

BEGINNING OF THE CHURCH
Ministry of the Apostles in
preaching and healing

PAUL'S MISSIONARY JOURNEYS
Gentiles receive the Gospel

PERSECUTION OF CHRISTIANS
By Jews and Roman Caesars

EMPEROR CONSTANTINE
MAKES CHRISTIANITY
LEGAL

ROMAN CATHOLIC CHURCH STRONG
THROUGHOUT WESTERN EUROPE

PROTESTANT REFORMATION BEGINS
Led by Martin Luther

GOSPEL SPREADS AROUND THE WORLD IN SPITE
OF PERSECUTION IN MANY COUNTRIES

JESUS RETURNS TO EARTH FOR A GLORIFIED CHURCH

Step 3

Bible References

Bible References

You've already taken two steps on the pathway of a good Bible student. You've learned to name the books of the Bible, and you know how the books are arranged. You even know a little about each book and its writer. By now, you should be feeling more comfortable with your wonderful Bible.

Are you ready for a new skill? Then we'll take another step. This one's about Bible references. When you have completed this step, you'll know how to read any Bible reference you might see in any book. You'll also know how to write them. Then, most important of all, you'll be able to find any reference in the Bible quickly and easily.

READING AND WRITING REFERENCES

Many years ago a group of Bible scholars went through the Bible and divided most of the books into *chapters* and gave each chapter a number. A few of the books are too short to be divided into chapters. Next, they divided the chapters into *verses* with numbers. This system makes it possible to "refer" to any part of the Bible by giving the name of the book, the number of the chapter, and the number of the verse. When this information is given, we call it a *Bible reference* or a *scripture reference*.

Printing companies that print Bibles have used many different styles for the pages of their Bibles. Some Bibles have each verse written separately. The number of the verse is given on the left side in the margin, and the first line is indented in each verse. This makes it easy to find a specific verse. In other Bibles, the verses are printed in paragraphs like other books. The numbers of the verses are printed at the beginning of the verses — in the middle of the line of print. The idea is that this makes it easier to read the stories. However, it may be a little harder to find a certain verse.

Study the samples on the next two pages. They're from different Bibles. Each one is from the third chapter of the Gospel of John. Read each one. Which is easier to read? To understand? Find verse 5. Which is easiest?

TO TAKE THIS STEP —
Learn the common abbreviations of the books of the Bible.

Learn to read and write any scripture reference.

Learn to locate any reference quickly and confidently.

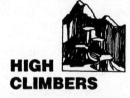

HIGH CLIMBERS

Practice reading all references on the Practice Sheet. Find and read them in the Bible.

CHAPTER 3

THERE was a man of the Pharisees, named Nĭc-o-dĕ'mus, a ruler of the Jews:

2 The same came to Jesus by night, and said unto him, Rabbi, we know that thou art a teacher come from God: for no man can do these miracles that thou doest, except God be with him.

3 Jesus answered and said unto him, Verily, verily, I say unto thee, Except a man be born again, he cannot see the kingdom of God.

4 Nĭc-o-dĕ'mus saith unto him, How can a man be born when he is old? can he enter the second time into his mother's womb, and be born?

5 Jesus answered, Verily, verily, I say unto thee, Except a man be born of water and of the Spirit, he cannot enter into the kingdom of God.

6 That which is born of the flesh is flesh; and that which is born of the Spirit is spirit.

7 Marvel not that I said unto thee, Ye must be born again.

8 The wind bloweth where it listeth, and thou hearest the sound thereof, but canst not tell whence it cometh, and whither it goeth: so is every one that is born of the Spirit.

9 Nĭc-o-dĕ'mus answered and said unto him, How can these things be?

KING JAMES VERSION
Thomas Nelson, Inc.

---

3 Now there was a man of the Pharisees, named Nicode'mus, a ruler of the Jews. 2 This man came to Jesus [d] by night and said to him, "Rabbi, we know that you are a teacher come from God; for no one can do these signs that you do, unless God is with him." 3 Jesus answered him, "Truly, truly, I say to you, unless one is born anew,[e] he cannot see the kingdom of God." 4 Nicode'mus said to him, "How can a man be born when he is old? Can he enter a second time into his mother's womb and be born?" 5 Jesus answered, "Truly, truly, I say to you, unless one is born of water and the Spirit, he cannot enter the kingdom of God. 6 That which is born of the flesh is flesh, and that which is born of the Spirit is spirit.[f] 7 Do not marvel that I said to you, 'You must be born anew.'[e] 8 The wind[f] blows where it wills, and you hear the sound of it, but you do not know whence it comes or whither it goes; so it is with every one who is born of the Spirit." 9 Nicode'mus said to him, "How can this be?" 10 Jesus an-

REVISED STANDARD VERSION
Thomas Nelson and Sons

CHAPTER 3

NOW there was a man of the Pharisees, named [a]Nicodemus, a [b]ruler of the Jews;

2 this man came to Him by night, and said to Him, "[a]Rabbi, we know that You have come from God *as* a teacher; for no one can do these [1b]signs that You do unless [c]God is with him."

3 Jesus answered and said to him, "Truly, truly, I say to you, unless one [a]is born [1]again, he cannot see [b]the kingdom of God."

4 Nicodemus *said to Him, "How can a man be born when he is old? He cannot enter a second time into his mother's womb and be born, can he?"

5 Jesus answered, "Truly, truly, I say to you, unless one is born of [a]water and the Spirit, he cannot enter into [b]the kingdom of God.

6 "[a]That which is born of the flesh is flesh; and that which is born of the Spirit is spirit.

7 "Do not marvel that I said to you, 'You must be born [1]again.'

8 "[a]The wind blows where it wishes and you hear the sound of it, but do not know where it comes from and where it is going; so is every one who is born of the Spirit."

9 Nicodemus answered and said to Him, "How can these things be?"

NEW AMERICAN STANDARD
A. J. Holman Company

CHAPTER 3

NOW there was a certain man among the Pharisees named Nicodemus, a ruler — a leader, an authority — among the Jews;

2 Who came to Jesus at night and said to Him, Rabbi, we know *and* are certain that You are come from God [as] a Teacher; for no one can do these signs — these wonderworks, these miracles, and produce the proofs — that You do, unless God is with him.

3 Jesus answered him, I assure you, most solemnly I tell you, that unless a person is born again (anew, from above), he cannot ever see — know, be acquainted with [and experience] — the kingdom of God.

4 Nicodemus said to Him, How can a man be born when he is old? Can he enter his mother's womb again, and be born?

5 Jesus answered, I assure you, most solemnly I tell you, except a man be born of water and (meven) the Spirit, he cannot [ever] enter the kingdom of God. [Ezek. 36:25-27.]

6 What is born of [from] the flesh is flesh — of the physical is physical; and what is born of the Spirit is spirit.

THE AMPLIFIED BIBLE
Zondervan Bible Publishers

3 AFTER DARK ONE night a Jewish religious leader named Nicodemus, a member of the sect of the Pharisees, came for an interview with Jesus. "Sir," he said, "we all know that God has sent you to teach us. Your miracles are proof enough of this."

[3]Jesus replied, "With all the earnestness I possess I tell you this: Unless you are born again, you can never get into the Kingdom of God."

[4]"Born again!" exclaimed Nicodemus. "What do you mean? How can an old man go back into his mother's womb and be born again?"

[5]Jesus replied, "What I am telling you so earnestly is this: Unless one is born of water[a] and the Spirit, he cannot enter the Kingdom of God. [6]Men can only reproduce human life, but the Holy Spirit gives new life from heaven; [7]so don't be surprised at my statement that you must be born again! [8]Just as you can hear the wind but can't tell where it comes from or where it will go next, so it is with the Spirit. We do not know on whom he will next bestow this life from heaven."

THE LIVING BIBLE
Tyndale House Publishers

CHAPTER 3

Jesus and a religious leader

1,2 ONE night Nicodemus, a leading Jew and a Pharisee, came to see Jesus.

"Master," he began, "we realise that you are a teacher who has come from God. Obviously no one could show the signs that you show unless God were with him."

3 "Believe me," returned Jesus, "a man cannot even see the kingdom of God without being born again."

4 "And how can a man who's getting old possibly be born?" replied Nicodemus. "How can he go back into his mother's womb and be born a second time?"

5 "I assure you," said Jesus, "that unless a man is born from water
6 and from spirit he cannot enter the kingdom of God. Flesh gives birth
7 to flesh and spirit gives birth to spirit: you must not be surprised that I
8 told you that all of you must be born again. The wind blows where it likes, you can hear the sound of it but you have no idea where it comes from and where it goes. Nor can you tell how a man is born by the wind of the Spirit."
9 "How on earth can things like this happen?" replied Nicodemus.
10 "So you are a teacher of Israel," said Jesus, "and you do not
11 recognise such things? I assure you that we are talking about something we really know and we are witnessing to something we

184

THE NEW TESTAMENT IN MODERN ENGLISH
J. B. Phillips
The MacMillan Company

Study these references and practice reading them.

John 3:16	Read:	*John, three, sixteen.*
	It means:	The book of John, the third chapter, the sixteenth verse.
John 3:16-21	Read:	*John, three, sixteen <u>through</u> twenty-one.*
	It means:	The book of John, the third chapter. Begin with verse 16 and read <u>to the end of</u> verse 21. You will read six verses.
John 3:16, 21	Read:	*John, three, sixteen <u>and</u> twenty-one.*
	It means:	The book of John, the third chapter. Use verse 16. Leave out all the verses between. Then read verse 21. Only two verses will be read.
Luke 8:50b	Read:	*Luke eight, fifty, b.*
	It means:	The book of Luke, the eighth chapter, the 50th verse, only the <u>last part</u> of the verse. A reference like this is usually used when that part of a verse is a familiar quotation. It is usually separated from the first part of the verse by some kind of punctuation.
I Corinthians 13:4	Read:	*First Corinthians, thirteen, four.*
	It means:	The first of the two books with the same name, Corinthians. Look for the thirteenth chapter and the fourth verse.

In some Bibles a different way is used to write references. Look at these. Be sure you can recognize and read each one either way.

I Jn. 3:18	may be written	1 Jn. 3.18
Psa. 1:6	may be written	Psa. 1.06
II Ki. 17:39	may be written	2 Ki. 17.39
Gen. 18:23-32	may be written	Gen. 18.23-32
Ro. 8:3	may be written	Ro. 8.3
Gal. 6:14	may be written	Gal. 6.14
Acts 10:28;11:3	may be written	Ac. 10.28;11.3

A LAMP UNTO MY FEET

The entrance of thy words giveth light; it giveth understanding unto the simple. (Psalm 119:130)

Did you have trouble reading the references on the last page? References are usually given with abbreviations of the books. Study this chart of abbreviations until you recognize them every time.

ABBREVIATIONS OF THE BOOKS OF THE BIBLE

This list was made from dictionaries and from several translations of the Bible. If you find others, add them to the list.

OLD TESTAMENT		NEW TESTAMENT	
Genesis	Gen., Ge.	Matthew	Matt., Mt., Ma., Mat., M't
Exodus	Ex., Exod.	Mark	Mk., M'k
Leviticus	Lev., Levit., Lv., Le.	Luke	Lk., Lu.
Numbers	Num., Nu.	John	Jno., Jn., Jo., Joh.
Deuteronomy	Deut., De., Dt.	Acts	Ac.
Joshua	Josh., Jos.	Romans	Rom., Ro.
Judges	Jud., J'g, Ju.	Corinthians	Cor., Co.
Ruth	Ru.	Galatians	Gal., Ga.
Samuel	Sam., Sa.	Ephesians	Eph., Ep., Ephes.
Kings	Ki., K., Kgs.	Philippians	Phil., Ph., Ph'p
Chronicles	Chron., Ch., Chr.	Colossians	Col.
Ezra	Ez., Ezr.	Thessalonians	Thess., Th.
Nehemiah	Neh., Ne.	Timothy	Tim., Ti.
Esther	Esth., Es.	Titus	Tit.
Job	Jb., Job	Philemon	Philem., Phile., Phm., Ph'm
Psalms	Ps., Psa.	Hebrews	Heb., Hebr., He.
Proverbs	Prov., Pr.	James	Ja., Jas., Jam.
Ecclesiastes	Eccles., Ecc., Ec., Eccl.	Peter	Pet., Pe.
Song of Solomon	S. of S., Sol., Song	Jude	Jde., Jude
Isaiah	Isa., Is.	Revelation	Rev., Re.
Jeremiah	Jer., Je.		
Lamentations	Lam., La.		
Ezekiel	Ezek., Eze.		
Daniel	Dan., Danl., Da., Dn.		
Hosea	Hos., Ho.		
Joel	Jl., Joe., Jo.		
Amos	Am.		
Obadiah	Ob., Obad.		
Jonah	Jon.		
Micah	Mic., Mi.		
Nahum	Nah., Na.		
Habakkuk	Hab.		
Zephaniah	Zeph., Zep., Zph.		
Haggai	Hag.		
Zechariah	Zech., Zec., Zch.		
Malachi	Mal.		

LOCATING REFERENCES

Many preachers and teachers tell their audiences which scripture they're using. This gives you a chance to look for that scripture in your own Bible and read it along with the speaker. It's a very good practice. You'll learn much more from the sermon or lesson if you can see the words.

With practice, you'll learn to find scripture references quickly and confidently. Here's a little information that will help you:

Pretend your Bible is divided into four sections. If you open it to the very middle, you should always find the book of *Psalms*. (Note: If your Bible has a section of study helps in the back, you may need to move to the left a bit more.)

If you open the left half to the middle, you should be in the book of *I Samuel*. If you open the right half to the middle, you should be in the book of *Matthew*. The entire New Testament is in the last quarter of the Bible.

Now, if you know the books of the Bible well, you can quickly turn to the quarter of the Bible in which any book is located and then find the scripture reference given.

Study this chart. Try to keep in mind which books are in the four parts. It will be very helpful to you.

Genesis Exodus Leviticus Numbers Deuteronomy Joshua Judges Ruth	I S A M U E L	II Samuel I Kings II Kings I Chronicles II Chronicles Ezra Nehemiah Esther Job	P S A L M S	Proverbs Ecclesiastes Song of Solomon Isaiah Jeremiah Lamentations Ezekiel Daniel Hosea Joel Amos Obadiah Jonah Micah Nahum Habakkuk Zephaniah Haggai Zechariah Malachi	M A T T H E W	All of the books of the New Testament

Step 4

The Bible's Own Story

The Bible's Own Story

You've now had many experiences with the Bible. You're becoming a more skillful Bible student as you take each new step. As you have worked with your Bible, you may have become curious about how this Book came to be the way it is. Wouldn't you like to know the answers to questions like these?

Were these the only books ever written?

Who decided which books would be in the Bible?

How did it come to be arranged the way it is?

Have any writings been added to the Bible since it was put together?

How can we be sure that it's really the Word of God?

Are there any mistakes in it?

One of the reasons people don't read the Bible more is that they aren't really sure they can believe it. Before the Bible can truly become the Word of God for you, it's absolutely necessary for you to know that it's from God. It's not just another book of history stories and thoughts of great men. It's actually God speaking to His people. Bible students must understand this.

In Step 4 you'll learn that our Bible has an exciting story of its very own. As we look at the history of the Bible, many of your questions will be answered. It's a story filled with adventure, danger, miracles, and heroes. You'll want to praise God for all the men and women who've made it possible for us to have the Bible to study.

TO TAKE THIS STEP —
Learn the names and terms on the review page.

HIGH CLIMBERS

Learn the names and terms on the review page AND the ones marked For High Climbers.

WHO WROTE THE BIBLE?

We often say that the Bible is the *Word of God.* And yet, as you've learned, it was written by men. How can this be? The Bible itself answers that question. We'll look at some of the scriptures that tell us so.

1. There are hundreds of places in the Old Testament where we can read words like these:

*And the Lord spake unto Moses, "Go unto Pharaoh, and say unto him, **Thus saith the Lord,** 'Let my people go, that they may serve me . . .'"*
(Exodus 8:1)

*For **thus saith the Lord God, the Holy One of Israel;** "In returning and rest shall ye be saved; in quietness and in confidence shall be your strength; and ye would not."* (Isaiah 30:15)

Over and over, in almost all of the Old Testament books, we find such statements. Look through the book of *Exodus* and count how many chapters begin with something like this: "And the Lord said unto Moses." You could do the same in the books of *Leviticus* and *Numbers.* Then you could turn to the books of the prophets and find that each one of them has said many times, "Thus saith the Lord."

2. Jesus, Himself, believed the writings of the Old Testament and quoted from them frequently. Read the Gospel stories and see how many times He refers to the prophets and the Law of Moses. One example is in *Luke.*

And he came to Nazareth,. . . and, as his

custom was, he went into the synagogue on the sabbath day, and stood up to read. And there was delivered unto him the book of the prophet, Isaiah. And when he had opened the book, he found the place where it was written . . . And he closed the book, . . . And he began to say unto them, "This day is this scripture fulfilled in your ears." (Luke 4:16-21)

A LAMP UNTO MY FEET

Forever, O Lord, thy word is settled in heaven. (Psalm 119:89)

While He was still with His disciples, Jesus made it clear to them that *His* words were to be remembered also. This makes them scripture for us just as much as the Old Testament writings were scripture for Jesus and the Jews of His time. Look at two references:

Jesus answered and said unto him, "If a man love me, he will keep my words: and my Father will love him, and we will come unto him, and make our abode with him. He that loveth me not keepeth not my sayings: and the word which ye hear is not mine, but the Father's which sent me." (John 14:23-24)

These words spake Jesus, and lifted up his eyes to heaven, and said . . . "Sanctify them through thy truth: thy word is truth . . . Neither pray I for these alone, but for them also which shall believe on me through their word." (John 17:1, 17, 20)

3. **The New Testament writers believed the writings of the Old Testament were from God.** Here are a few scriptures that make us know this:

Knowing this first, that no prophecy of the scripture is of any private interpretation. For the prophecy came not in old time by the will of man: but holy men of God spake as they were moved by the Holy Ghost. (II Peter 1:20-21)

All scripture is given by inspiration of God, and is profitable for doctrine, for reproof, for correction, for instruction in righteousness: That the man of God may be perfect, thoroughly furnished unto all good works. (II Timothy 3:16-17)

From these two apostles, we learn that the scriptures were *inspired* by God. That word really means "God-breathed." It tells us that God spoke to them, and they wrote what He wanted them to say. Paul wanted Timothy to know that he could put his trust in the scriptures. And that is what Peter was telling us in his letter. The writer of Hebrews also told us we could believe that God spoke to us through His Son.

God, who at various times and in different ways spoke in time past to the fathers by the prophets, has in these last days spoken to us by His Son, whom He has appointed heir of all things, by whom also He made the worlds. . . (Hebrews 1:1-2 New KJV)

Who wrote the Bible? Men inspired by the Holy Spirit.

Why can we believe this? Because Jesus and all the New Testament writers believed it. If they believed it, then we can believe it, too.

50

HOW WAS THE BIBLE WRITTEN?

Bibles are everywhere. We can go to almost any store where books are sold and find a Bible. You may have several Bibles in your home. There are many different kinds of Bibles. Most of them have black leather bindings, and they often have pages with gold edges. (Of course, there are other colors, too.) Inside, you may find the scriptures printed on very thin paper. There may be pictures of scenes from the stories.

Bibles weren't always like this, however. Nearly 40 different men wrote the books of the Bible and it took over 1,000 years. Yet, not one of their writings looked like the Bibles we use today. In fact, you would think they looked very strange. You wouldn't be able to read even one word. Let's take a look at these early "books."

WRITING MATERIALS

The Old Testament writers wrote in Hebrew. That was the language of the people of their time. They wrote on a material called papyrus (pah PĪ rus). Some wrote on parchment. It's good that they had materials like this because papyrus and parchment could last many years if they were cared for properly. It's also a good thing that the climate in that part of the world is very dry. Moisture might have caused the materials to decay much faster.

Papyrus

Our word "paper" comes from the word "papyrus." Papyrus is the name of a plant that grows in the Nile River Valley in Egypt. It has long straight stalks with three sides, like a triangle. There's a kind of bristle that sticks out at the top, but the plant doesn't have leaves.

The writing material was made from the stalk of the plant, which was cut into sections. The length of these sections depended on how wide the "paper" was supposed to be. The tough, green, outer layer was stripped off the stalk. Then the

inner part (pith) was sliced into thin strips, and a sticky substance oozed from them. The strips were laid side by side, overlapping, slightly, to make a single layer. A second layer was laid on top of the first one, but it was placed in the opposite direction. Then these layers were pounded with a heavy mallet to make them begin to fuse together. Next, the entire piece was carefully laid between squares of linen cloth and squares of wool. Pressure was applied, usually by placing a large stone on top. The linen cloths were changed often, because they became soaked with the substance from the strips. After several days of this changing and pressure from the stone, the papyrus strips became fused together into a thin, single sheet. It was white and limp at first, but gradually it became crisp and light brown from exposure to the air. These small sheets were usually joined together to make one long sheet. Some of them were many feet long. One has been found that was over 100 feet in length. The shorter ones could be folded, but longer ones were rolled. Sometimes they were attached to rods to make rolling them easier. These were called "scrolls."

Papyrus Letter
Folded, tied, and sealed

The Egyptians were very skillful at making papyrus writing material. They sold it to other countries around the Mediterranean Sea for hundreds of years. There were great collections of scrolls. When the Greeks came, they built libraries with thousands and thousands of scrolls in them in some of their large cities.

Parchment

Parchment was first made by the Greeks about 200 years before the time of Christ. When one of the Egyptian kings became jealous of the Greek libraries, he refused to sell the Greeks any more papyrus. He didn't want them to have libraries larger than his own. So the Greeks had to find something else for writing material. They began to experiment with animal skins, and finally, they developed parchment.

The animals used for this material were usually sheep and goats. It could take as many as 25 sheep to make one scroll. Sometimes other animals were used — donkeys, antelopes, wolves, or calves. The parchment was made by removing the hair or wool from the animal skin and stretching the skin very thin. A white powder was rubbed into it to make it soft.

The best quality of parchment was made from young animals — kids, lambs, calves. This is called *vellum* (VEL uhm). It was very expensive. That's why it was used for only the most important documents.

Parchment lasts much longer than papyrus. Even today, important documents are written on parchment. The laws of the United States, for example, are on parchment. Regular paper would crumble away after a few years.

Sheets of parchment were difficult to join together to make scrolls, but the Greeks discovered that they could attach the sheets along one side by sewing them together. This was called a *codex* (KŌ deks). It was the beginning of books with pages. Gradually, better and better ways of binding sheets together were developed.

Scrolls

A scroll (skrōl) was a long sheet of papyrus (or other writing material) which had a wooden rod attached to each end. The paper wound around the rods as they were turned toward the center of the sheet. Sometimes ivory or bronze was used for the rods. The ends of the rods that stuck out from the writing material were often made into knobs or handles. They protected the edges of the papyrus roll and helped the reader handle the heavy scroll. Sometimes they were beautifully decorated.

A LAMP UNTO MY FEET

If ye continue in my word, then are ye my disciples indeed; And ye shall know the truth, and the truth shall make you free. (John 8:31b-32)

The Hebrews still use scrolls for their ancient writings. Their most sacred ones are kept in cases with hinges. The cases may be made of wood or leather or metal. Many are covered with heavy cloth and decorated with much gold and silver.

Many scrolls have an interesting little pointer. This is a metal stick tied to the end of one of the rods with a ribbon or cord. On the end of the stick is a very tiny bronze or gold or silver "hand" which has a tiny pointing finger. When the reader uses the scrolls, he uses the little hand to follow along the line and help him keep his place. He reads the Hebrew writing from right to left.

Pen and Ink

Since the time that man learned to write, he has managed to find some kind of material with which to put it down. At first, he probably used a sharp piece of bone or a stick to scratch on stone or soft clay. Later, he covered a piece of wood with a layer of wax. When papyrus was invented, he needed ink. He learned how to mix the soot from burned bricks or lamps with a little oil. This worked well, and he could have it with little cost or effort. The Egyptians sharpened a hollow reed to use for a pen. Other people used feathers. These were called *quills*. Goose quills were best, and they were used for writing until late in the 1800s.

It's surprising how well the ink lasted on the old parchment scrolls. Since parchment was expensive, it was sometimes used more than once. The old ink would be taken off and new writing put on. And yet, Bible scholars who have found such copies have been able to take off the top writing and read the original copy. In many cases, the first writing was far more valuable to us than the second.

THE WORK OF THE SCRIBES

The work of those inspired men who first wrote down the word of God was very important. The scrolls on which they wrote were probably protected very carefully. And yet, not one of the original writings has ever been found. The scrolls that have been found are copies of copies of copies. Even those copies are from many centuries later than the originals. How can we be sure our scripture is what was first written? Is it possible that mistakes were made in the copying somewhere? This is why we must study about the work of the scribes. You'll see that we owe them a great deal of gratitude for what they did for us.

The scribes who copied the scriptures were usually the best educated men of their time. They were greatly respected. Many had the important task of keeping public records. Every king hired many scribes to write down the events of the kingdom and prepare royal announcements.

In ancient Israel some of the scribes had the job of copying the Law (or Torah). As you remember, this is the first five books of our Bible. The scribes considered it a sacred duty and worked hard to copy accurately. Later, scribes copied the writings of the prophets and the Wisdom Literature.

The scribes were very skillful, but they still made mistakes sometimes. We know it is impossible for anyone to copy so much

Working in a Scriptorium

any mistakes? These men did it all day.

About 500 years after Christ, a group of people called *Massoretes* (MAS ō rēts) took over the copying of the Old Testament manuscripts. These men were well-trained and took great care to copy exactly. Just to be sure they had not left out letters or added extra ones, they counted the letters on each page. The Massoretes also added dots and lines under the consonants to show where vowel sounds should be. They corrected the mistakes which had shown up in earlier **manuscripts,** too. Their text became the Hebrew Old Testament that was finally printed and handed down to us.

Can you see that the copyists had to be inspired by God just as much as the first writers? We know their manuscripts were accurate. There are hundreds of copies now in existence, so it's easy to compare one with another to prove it.

material by hand without making at least a few mistakes. By the time of the first printing press in A.D. 1456, all scriptures had been copied and recopied for over 1,000 years. Some went back for 3,000 years.

The Hebrew language made it even more difficult to copy. There were no vowels or spaces between words. If our English language were like that, Psalm 23:1 would look like this:

THLRDSMSHPHRDSHLLNTWNT

Many scribes worked alone, copying and copying day after day. Sometimes, the scribes worked in a *scriptorium*. This was a room in which there might be a dozen or more men sitting at desks. Each one might be making a parchment copy from a papyrus scroll. He had to copy one letter at a time, looking from copy to copy. In some places, a reader sat at a desk in the front of the room and read the scripture aloud very slowly. All the men listened and wrote down the words they heard. There was absolutely no talking or noise of any kind. How easy it would have been to make mistakes! Perhaps they couldn't hear the words clearly. Or they might get sleepy and get behind. Could *you* copy for even one hour without talking at all? Could you copy one page of material without making

The Dead Sea Scrolls and Qumran (KOOM rahn)

Sometimes scribes would risk their lives to copy the scriptures and keep them safe. One example of this was a group of Jews called the *Essenes* (ES ēnz). These people lived about the time that Jesus was here on earth. Some of them gave all their time and attention to the copying of the Old Testament. In order to be undisturbed in their work, one group of Essenes built a small community near the Dead Sea in southern Israel.

For most of us, it would be unpleasant to live there. It's a desert region with no green grass or trees or bushes. Nearby are high rocky cliffs with many caves. The only

---

WORDS TO KNOW

manuscript (MAN ū skript) — *book or paper written by hand.*

water they had was what they could catch from the spring rains in stone tanks called cisterns.

The ruins of their small community still stand today. One of the buildings was a scriptorium where the scribes worked on the manuscripts. We know this because a table and inkwells with dried ink still in them were found there. Another building was a workshop where the people made large clay jars in which to store the manuscripts.

In A.D. 68, the Roman army marched across Israel. When the Essenes heard the Romans were coming, they acted very quickly. Their beloved manuscripts were sealed into the large clay jars and taken to the caves in the cliffs. When the Roman

army came, the people were all killed, but the scriptures were safely hidden.

There is evidence that an earthquake shook the area at one point in history since that time, but the caves kept their precious secret.

In fact, the manuscripts weren't found until early spring of 1947.

In the spring, there's enough rain in Israel to cause some grass to sprout. A few shepherds take their sheep and goats to graze in this area near the Dead Sea. That spring, one young shepherd lost a goat in the rugged hills and went to find it. He saw

one of the caves and thought the goat might have fallen into it, so he threw a stone into the hole. When he heard the sound of breaking pottery, he climbed down to see what it was. On the floor of the cave he saw some large clay jars. In the broken ones he could see leather scrolls. He took some of the jars and scrolls to a shopkeeper in Jerusalem. This man kept them in a room over his shop for several months before he told anyone else. Finally, however, the scrolls reached the hands of a Bible scholar. Since that time they have been studied by many people.

More scrolls were found in other caves. All the scrolls had been kept in very good condition for over 1,900 years. One scroll was the whole book of Isaiah. It was 10 inches wide and 24 feet long. Parts of almost all the books of the Old Testament were found in the caves. These precious scrolls are called the *Dead Sea Scrolls*. They're important because they're the oldest copies of scriptures that have been discovered. Also, when they were compared with the Massorete copies, only a few little unimportant differences were found. This helps us to feel even more confident about our scriptures. Now we know that they are as accurate as they can possibly be.

Because these scrolls mean so much to so many people, a special building was built for them in Jerusalem. It was made in the shape of the top of the clay jar in which the first scroll was found. It's called the *Shrine of the Book*. Visitors can see the scrolls there. They are kept under glass in a room where the temperature is kept just right to preserve them. To enter the building, you must go down into a cave-like room. This is to remind you of the place where they were found.

Next to the white dome of the museum is a large, shiny black wall built in memory of all the Jewish people who have suffered for their beliefs over the years.

Shrine of the Book

THE WORK OF THE ARCHAEOLOGIST

We are also grateful for the work of the archaeologists (AR ki OL uh jists). It's their work that has given us much of our information about Bible times. More and more, their discoveries are showing us that the Bible stories are true. Archaeologists are at work throughout the Bible world. Their work is very interesting, but it's also quite difficult. Often they must live in tents without much comfort for months at a time. Some spend their entire lives at their work. What, exactly, do archaeologists do?

Tel el Hesi

All over Israel there are places called *tells*. Tells look like ordinary hills, but they're not. Archaeologists know that there are ruins of ancient cities in those hills.

In ancient times, before nations developed, most people lived in groups called *tribes*. These tribes were made up of the many generations of a large family, including their slaves and a few strangers who had come to live among them. There was always fighting among different tribes. Because of this, the people had to look for a place to live that would be easy to defend in time of war. In Palestine, the best place was usually the highest place in a region. If a tribe could find a slight rise with flat land around it, the people would build their town on top of it.

Homes were built with bricks made from the clay of a nearby stream. Then the people went about their daily lives. They planted, harvested and stored crops. Their tools and weapons were very simple. They always had a great deal of pottery because they used it for every possible daily need. Each community made its pottery a little different from the others, and the styles changed over the centuries.

Eventually, something would happen to the town. It might be a fire or a disease that would take many lives. Usually, it was war. The remaining people would move to another place.

For many years the dirt and sand would blow across the deserted town. Roofs caved in. Winter rains washed dirt into the rooms of the little houses. After a time, the town would be completely buried. Along would come another tribe looking for a place to build. Finding the hill, they would begin their homes.

This happened many times over the centuries. One town built over another that was buried under their own. The hill, of course, became higher and higher.

Now, in the 20th century, an archaeologist looks at one of those hills and recognizes it as a tell. He knows that ancient people once lived there. Under the soil he finds walls of houses, simple tools, and much pottery. He calls such things

56

artifacts. These artifacts give us many clues about those ancient people:

—who they were
—when they lived there
—how they lived their daily lives (even what foods they ate)
—how they fought their wars
—what kind of crops they grew
—and countless other facts

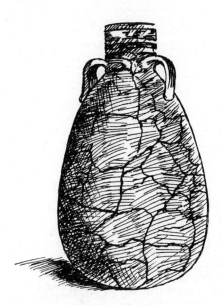

The archaeologist's task is to get the soil out of the way. But he mustn't lose any of the valuable artifacts or destroy any of the buildings under the soil. This takes a great deal of skill and hard work and patience. Sometimes he uses college students to help him. They mark off one square at a time and very carefully start taking out the dirt. Every day, as they dig deeper, they fill buckets with pieces of broken pottery, called *sherds.* The archaeologist studies these sherds for clues. Important pieces are given a number, and a record is made of them in a book. Sometimes most of the pieces of a whole vase or jar are found. A very skillful worker puts it back together like working a puzzle. You may have seen some restored pottery in a museum.

In some cases the dirt that is taken from a square is sifted through a screen to make sure they don't miss some small, valuable artifact like a bead or a coin. Drawings are made and photographs are taken after

each day's work. Then the archaeologist in charge will write all the information into books for others to study.

HOW DID "THE BOOKS" BECOME "THE BOOK"?

To answer this question we must learn some new words: *canon* (KAN uhn) and *canonizing.* The word "canon" means "a list of books thought to be inspired by God." The word "canonizing" means "the bringing together of such a list." In our Bible we have two canons — the Old Testament Canon and the New Testament Canon. They came to be canonized at different times and in different ways. Therefore, we are going to look at them separately.

THE OLD TESTAMENT CANON

Most of the books of the Old Testament were considered sacred from the time they were written. The Book of Moses (Torah or Pentateuch) was written about 1400 B.C. This section was not only the first, but it was also the most important. For the Jews, it still is today. Then came the prophets and other writings. Most of them were treasured by the Jews from the beginning. There never was any question about their being from God. The list kept growing until

about 400 B.C., when the book of the prophet Malachi was written.

Between 200 B.C. and A.D. 100, other writings appeared. Some Jews accepted them, but many didn't believe they were inspired by God. In A.D. 90, an important meeting called the *Council of Jamnia,* was held. At this Council, the Jewish leaders established the limits of the Hebrew canon. It included the 39 books of our Old Testament just as we have them today. Malachi was the latest book to be included. All the newer books were left out. There were just too many questions about them. That group of books is called the *Apocrypha* (uh POK ri fuh). The Roman Catholic Church, in later years, decided that these books should have been included. The Protestant Church has preferred to leave them out. That is why you won't usually find them in Protestant Bibles, but you will find them in Catholic Bibles. Some Bible students like to read them to learn more about the history of the period between the Old and New Testaments. When they're added to a Bible, they're usually printed between the Testaments.

THE NEW TESTAMENT CANON

When the Gospels and letters of the New Testament began to appear, they were sent from church to church. Scribes made copies so that more churches could have them. They were copied and recopied. Eventually, the originals were lost. However, with so many copies around, it was possible to keep checking and comparing to find errors and correct them.

Some Bible scholars spend a great deal of time and effort looking for the old manuscripts. When one is found, it becomes a treasure and is carefully protected, as you learned with the Dead Sea Scrolls. Each discovery would be an

exciting story. The oldest New Testament manuscript that we have is the *Vatican Codex.* It's called this because it is in the Vatican Museum in Rome. It's written on vellum in Greek capital letters. This kind of writing is called *uncials* (UHN si uhls). This manuscript contains all of the Old and New Testaments. Remember, a codex is not a scroll. It has sheets of writing material sewn together at the edge.

Codex Sinaiticus

Another important manuscript is the *Sinai Codex.* It has an interesting story. It was discovered in a monastery on Mt. Sinai (the mountain where Moses was given the Ten Commandments hundreds of years earlier). A man from Germany, named Tischendorf (TISH en dorf), was looking for old manuscripts. His study had given him the idea that there were some writings at this monastery. When he went there, he found that the only way in and out was by climbing a rope. He had trouble getting the men of the monastery to let him climb up. Finally, however, he was allowed to go in. Then they didn't want to help him look for manuscripts. Just as he was about to leave, he saw some vellum pages in a basket of things to be burned. When he saw what they were, he talked the men into letting him take 43 pages with him. He knew there must be more of

---

WORDS TO KNOW   council (KOWN sil) — *a group of people called together to settle questions.*

them somewhere at the monastery. It took many years, but he succeeded in getting the help he needed to buy all of the manuscript. It was brought together and is in the British Museum in London today.

The New Testament canon wasn't fixed until the fourth century. By this time, there had been a great many writings. There were also people coming into the churches who were teaching things that were wrong. They didn't agree with the teachings of the early apostles. The apostles were men who had been with Jesus and had been taught by Him personally. Any teaching that didn't agree with theirs was not to be accepted.

In A.D. 303, a Roman ruler passed a law demanding that all sacred Christian books be destroyed. Some Christians were giving their lives to protect these books. It was time for a decision to be made about what was inspired by God and what was not. The first list of the 27 books as we have them in our Bible was found in a letter written in A.D. 367. Thirty years later, the *Council of Carthage* decided that these same 27 books would be the New Testament Canon. It has never changed.

It is good to know that the Holy Spirit was inspiring the Church leaders in both of these councils. They made the selection of the books that have become our Holy Bible.

HOW DID THE BIBLE GET INTO OTHER LANGUAGES?

The Greek language was spoken in all the countries of the Bible world. It began to spread to other countries during the time of the warrior ruler Alexander the Great. He conquered many countries in Africa and Asia. Before long, Greek ideas and ways began showing up everywhere. Long before Christ came, many Hebrew people had moved to other countries. Like everyone else, they learned to speak Greek. Many of them couldn't even read

Hebrew anymore. This made them want to have their sacred scriptures in the Greek language.

Hebrew Pentateuch

Seventy men were chosen to come to a meeting. These men **translated** the Torah into Greek. The rest of the Old Testament was gradually translated as well. This Old Testament in Greek was called the *Septuagint* (sep TOO uh jint). It comes from the word for "seventy." The Septuagint became quite popular. It was probably the book used by the New Testament writers and read in the early Church. The Greek language had to add vowels and spaces between words, and this made it much longer than the Hebrew copy. It was necessary to use two scrolls for some of the longer books. That explains why we have two books of Samuel and Kings and Chronicles.

More years went by. The Roman army conquered the countries around the Mediterranean Sea. The language of the Romans was Latin. In Rome, a man called Jerome was asked to translate the Scriptures into Latin. To do this work, he went away from Rome and lived in Bethlehem in Israel. It took him 15 years. He worked from Hebrew and Greek manuscripts. Then he went back to Rome and presented his translation to the Church. At first the Christians did not like the Latin Bible and would not accept it. Jerome died broken-hearted. A few years later, however, it was not only accepted but became their official Latin Bible. It was called the *Latin Vulgate*. The word "vulgate" means "everyday speech." It was probably this Bible that was read by our English forefathers.

THE DARK AGES

The countries of Europe entered a period of nearly 1,000 years called the Dark Ages. From A.D. 500 to 1500, there was almost constant fighting all over Europe. Because of this, little or no learning took place. Very few people could read or write, so books weren't important to most of them. The precious scripture manuscripts seemed to disappear.

And yet, God wouldn't let this happen. Here and there, around western Europe, were groups of men who loved God and wanted to serve Him. They were called *monks*, and they went to live in places called *monasteries* far away from the towns. Do you remember reading about the one on Mt. Sinai?

Many of these men were skillful at writing. They spent their lives copying page after page of scripture. They worked long hours in very uncomfortable conditions. They had poor light, and the tiny rooms in which they worked were cold in winter and hot in summer. In spite of this, they tried to make their work the best it could possibly be. They began to make their copies beautiful as well. Around the margins they painted designs in red and blue and gold. Sometimes the first letter of a page or chapter would be made very large. The letter would then be surrounded with tiny angels or birds or perhaps a whole scene from the story. These decorated manuscripts were said to be "illuminated." Even in the Dark Ages, God was keeping His Word alive. It was the one bright light that still shone in the darkness.

An Illumination

HOW DID THE BIBLE GET INTO ENGLISH?

It was still a very long time before Bibles would look like the ones we have today. The English language didn't even look like it does today. You wouldn't be able to read the first English Bible. Before there were any translations into English, there were short paraphrases of Bible stories. A *paraphrase* (PAIR uh frāz) is a part of scripture that has been said in a different way from the original, but it means the same.

There's an interesting story about the first paraphrases in English. It's about a man named Caedmon (KAD mun) who took care of the cows at a monastery in Whitby, England. Poor Caedmon was ashamed that he didn't have talent like the other monks. Sometimes, after the evening meal in the banquet hall, they would take turns singing or playing musical instruments. One night he felt so embarrassed that he ran from the hall and hid in the stable. While there, he had a vision of the Lord. The Lord spoke to Caedmon.

"Sing me a song," He said.

"I cannot sing," said Caedmon. "That's why I came out here tonight."

"Yet shall you sing to me," said the Lord.

"What shall I sing?" asked Caedmon.

"Sing of the beginning of things," said the Lord.

The next day, Caedmon sang a paraphrase for the monks. They were amazed. From that time on, they would translate the Latin stories into English for him. Immediately, he would paraphrase them. Sometimes he would sing them with musical accompaniment. He not only sang about the Creation, but the history of Israel and the life of Jesus, too. The people loved it because it made the Bible stories easy for them to understand.

Very Early English

We know about Caedmon because of the writing of a man named Bede (bēd). He was a great scholar and wrote great things for England. One of the most important things he did was to translate many books of the Old and New Testaments into an early form of English. Caedmon lived in the 600s and Bede lived in the 700s.

The Bible carries the story of God's love for all human beings. It's a message of life and peace and joy. Every person needs to hear this message. And yet, it has taken many miracles for it to reach us. As the years passed, the Roman Catholic Church became very strong in Europe and England. Many leaders of the Church were greedy for power and money. They weren't interested in real Christianity. Only the Church leaders and a few rich people could have a Bible. At church services, the Bible was read in Latin and only a few people knew Latin. The leaders wanted the people to depend upon the Church for everything. They didn't want the people to read or hear the Bible. "It's too sacred for the common man," they said.

JOHN WYCLIFFE

In the 1300s a man named John Wycliffe grew up in England. He became a teacher at Oxford University. When he saw what the Church was doing, he wanted to do something about it. He started making speeches about the bad things that were going on in the Church. Of course, this made the leaders very angry.

They became even more upset when Wycliffe sent a group of preachers from town to town to read the Bible aloud to the

A LAMP UNTO MY FEET

But without faith it is impossible to please him: for he that cometh to God must believe that he is, and that he is a rewarder of them that diligently seek him. (Hebrews 11:6)

people. Then he started translating the Latin scriptures into English. He wanted the people to hear the Bible in their own language. Before long, his friends started making copies of his English translation. The common people were very excited about the "new" Bible. The king and the Church leaders hated Wycliffe. A law was passed which said, "No person may keep, copy, buy, or sell anything written by John Wycliffe." Any person who broke this law would be put to death.

Wycliffe kept right on translating until he died in the year 1384. About 100 years later, an angry bishop dug up Wycliffe's bones and burned them in the public square. He hoped the people would see what a bad person John Wycliffe had been. But the people had the Bible, and no one could make them hate the man who had given it to them.

THE PRINTING PRESS

The Bible could now be read in English, but only a few people could afford one. Copying was still expensive and slow. It took even the skillful scribes four or five months to copy a 200-page text. All the time, there were people trying to find a cheaper way to have books. Some carved words on blocks of wood and spread ink on them. Then they pressed the block onto a sheet of paper. It was messy and slow, but more than one copy could be made this way.

Finally, a man named Johann Gutenberg (YŌ hahn GOO ten berg) figured out a way to do it better. He lived in Strassburg, Germany. When he was still a young man, he started working in the printing business. He had good ideas, but he didn't have any money with which to buy supplies to try his ideas. To keep going, he often had to borrow money. He kept getting more and more in debt. And yet, he knew his idea would work. He made metal letters from a mold. This made it possible to make as many letters as he needed. In 1450 he began printing the world's first book, using movable type.

It was a Latin Bible. It took him five years. The job was still slow. The words for each page had to be spelled out, inked, and pressed onto the paper. After that, the titles and beginning letters were printed in red by hand. But there were 200 copies! He printed 35 on vellum and 165 on a cheaper kind of paper. Each Bible had 641 pages.

Gutenberg spent every penny he had on this project. The vellum and paper alone cost over $500. That was a great deal of money in those days. When he died, he was very poor and left many debts. And yet, the whole world owes him more than we could possibly pay. Think about Gutenberg the next time you read something.

WILLIAM TYNDALE

More and better printing presses were being used in Europe all the time. Back in England, a man named William Tyndale (TIN duhl) was studying Greek. One day he was using a Greek New Testament for practice. As he read, he began to see that this was not just another Greek book. It was truly the Word of God. And yet, he never saw the priests of the Church reading it. When he asked them about it, they said, "We had better be without God's laws than the Pope's."

Tyndale knew that this attitude wasn't right. He replied, "If God will spare me, I will one day make the boy that drives the plow in England to know more of Scripture than the Pope himself."

He began to translate the New Testament from Greek to English. He knew it was too dangerous to do his work in England. Therefore, he moved to Hamburg, Germany. Finally, after a year of very hard work, his first copy was ready for the printer, and he took it to the city of Cologne to be printed. He had kept his work a secret until now, but a priest found out from the printers what was going on at the print shop. A New Testament in English was being printed and it was almost completed. The priest quickly went to report this news to the bishop. Then they went to get the local law officers to arrest Tyndale and take away his New Testament.

But God performed a miracle, and Tyndale found out about their plans. He rushed to the print shop, snatched all the sheets from the presses, and ran with them. He found a print shop in another city, and the job was finished there. When the very first printed English New Testament came off the press, there were 3,000 of them! There was no stopping it now.

Getting the copies back to the people in England was another problem, however. The king had men waiting at every port to grab the Bibles and burn them. And yet, hundreds of copies kept getting through to the people. They were hidden in sacks of grain and bundles of cloth and other kinds of cargo. They were being bought almost as fast as they were unloaded. Almost anyone could afford to have a Bible now.

The Bishop of London thought he had a way to get rid of the Bibles. One of his rich friends went to the dock and paid for every copy that came in. Then he had them burned. This didn't stop the Bibles, though. Instead, Tyndale used the money to print even more.

Knowing he was no longer safe in Germany, Tyndale moved to Antwerp, Belgium. The people in that city were in favor of what he was doing and helped him every way they could. He began translating the Old Testament into English. But the king of England hired two men to find Tyndale and arrest him. They found him living in a house in Antwerp. The two men rented rooms in the same house and became friends to Tyndale. Soon they had enough proof, and he was put in prison.

Tyndale stayed in prison for over a year before he was even tried for his "crime." In 1536 he was finally tried, and he was burned at the stake. Before he died, he prayed, "O Lord, open the King of England's eyes." Do you know what Tyndale meant by that prayer?

MILES COVERDALE

Before Tyndale died, he had almost finished translating the Old Testament. Others were working on translations, too. A man named Miles Coverdale was one of these. He used Tyndale's work and finished in 1535, the same year Tyndale went to prison. Coverdale's was the first whole Bible to be printed in English.

Things were changing in England. King Henry VIII saw a copy of Coverdale's Bible and liked it. He gave an order that one large Bible should be placed in every church for the people to read. Tyndale's prayer was answered.

Every person who could buy a Bible had a copy. Everyone who could read was reading it. People who could not read would crowd around the Bible at the church, and it would be read aloud to them. Even boys and girls would sit quietly among the others to hear the Holy Scriptures. People wanted to learn to read just so they could read the Bible.

THE GREAT BIBLE

That wasn't the end of trouble for the Bible, however. There were more translations and more brave heroes. When Tyndale was sent to prison in 1535, he gave his translating work to a friend, John Rogers. This man was later arrested and burned at the stake, too.

A few years later, in 1539, another version was printed. It was the work of Miles Coverdale. The printing presses in France were better than those of England, and the work was begun there. It had been approved by the French king, but the Church stopped the printing and took what had already been finished. Therefore, the work was moved to England and completed. It was printed on pages 11 by 16 1/2 inches. Can you see why it was called the *Great Bible*? A copy was chained to the reading desk in each church in England. It became a very popular version.

Still, the Bible had more battles to fight. Church leaders persuaded King Henry to change his mind about the Bible. A law was passed to keep people from reading anything with Tyndale's name on it.

During Edward VI's short time as king, he tried to help the people get Bibles. Then came Queen Mary, a Roman Catholic. While she ruled, she tried to stop anyone or anything that was against the Roman Catholic Church. Hundreds of people were put to death during her rule.

THE GENEVA BIBLE

Coverdale escaped to Geneva, Switzerland. He worked with a group of Bible scholars for two and a half years to complete another Bible. When they finished in 1560, their Geneva Bible was the first complete English Bible to be divided into verses. It quickly became the favorite Bible in England and Scotland. This was the Bible of the Pilgrims who came to America. Now the Bible had crossed the ocean, and it was very important in the settling of the New World.

THE KING JAMES VERSION

Why do we have a Bible named for a king of England? The King James Version has been the most popular English Bible for over 300 years. The history of this translation is quite interesting. If you have one and read from it, you should know its story.

King James Version
1611

King James I called a meeting of Church leaders soon after he became king. They met in January of 1604 at a large palace near London called Hampton Court. They were there to discuss some Church problems. One decision that was made was that they needed a new translation of the Bible. King James liked the idea very much. He chose 47 of the best Bible scholars in England.

These men divided themselves into six groups, called panels. Each panel was given a certain part of the Bible to translate. Three panels took the Old Testament, two took the New Testament, and another translated the Apocrypha.

The scholars met in three large universities. They weren't paid for this work, so they had to continue to work at their regular jobs, also.

Before they started, they decided on certain rules to guide them. They would use other Bible translations: Tyndale, Coverdale, the Great Bible, the Geneva Bible, and one called the Bishop's Bible. They also used all the Greek and Hebrew manuscripts they could get.

Each panel finished its work. Then, two men from each panel went to a meeting. Each part of the entire Bible translation was read, word by word. As the others listened, if anyone wanted to make a change, it was worked out together. All of this took four years — from 1607 to 1611. The first copy was printed in 1611.

This 1611 King James Version isn't actually the one we read today, however. In fact, you wouldn't be able to read that first one. It has been revised several times. The spelling of words and the way we speak have changed over the years. In 1739, it was revised again, and this is the one we still use.

Now another revision of the King James Version has been made. In 1976 the process was begun. Over 100 people did the work. The language was changed to leave off the "eth" endings and to change the "thee" and "thou" pronouns to "you."

NEWER VERSIONS

The translators of the King James Version wanted their Bible to say just what the first writers wanted it to say. They used all the old manuscripts they had. However, older manuscripts have been found since then that are even closer to the originals. Many people said, "We need to make a translation from these earlier copies. It would be more accurate." Between 1611 and 1881 there were many translations. Most of them were made by individuals or small groups.

In 1885 in England, a complete Bible was published called the *Revised Version.* Much of the translating was done from the earlier Greek and Hebrew manuscripts and not from the earlier Bibles. In 1901 this same version came out in America. It was called the *American Standard Version.* It used American spelling and expressions where they were different from the British.

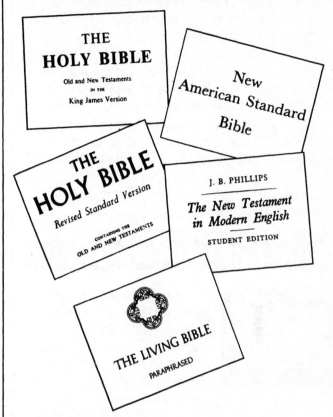

Later, in 1952, the *Revised Standard Version* was published. This group of translators wanted to make their translation even easier to read and understand. They arranged the text into paragraphs. Many people liked this new Bible, and it is used by many Americans today.

The Living Bible is not a translation. It is a paraphrase. The writer did not try to make it exactly like the original. He wanted to keep the meaning but say it in modern speech. He used expressions and terms that people in this time would understand. This Bible is sold everywhere in America. It is easy to read and sounds like a story book.

It seems that the Holy Spirit has inspired many translators and many revisers of the Scriptures. And yet, the King James Version is still the one most people read and memorize.

WHICH BIBLE IS RIGHT?

Which one of all these Bibles is the right one for you? The answer to that is, *"the one you will read."* It doesn't matter which version you choose if you aren't going to read it. If you enjoy reading from a certain version, you will likely pick up your Bible and read. If you find a particular version difficult to read or to understand, you won't read it. Only what you read and understand can help you. Make up your mind that you're going to read the Word of God. Ask the Holy Spirit to help you understand what you read. Then decide to live by it every day.

A LAMP UNTO MY FEET

For whatsoever things were written aforetime were written for our learning, that we through patience and comfort of the scriptures might have hope. (Romans 15:4)

INTO ALL THE WORLD

When Jesus was about to go back to His Father, He gave His disciples one last command:

> *But ye shall receive power, after that the Holy Ghost is come upon you: and ye shall be witnesses unto me both in Jerusalem, and in all Judea, and in Samaria, and unto the uttermost part of the earth.* (Acts. 1:8)

The Gospel message is for everyone. When a person accepts Jesus Christ as his Savior, he wants others to know about Jesus, too. Those early believers gave their lives to spread the Good News that Jesus saves us from our sins. And this same message is still being preached all over the world.

Those who receive the message need the written Word to help them to grow as Christians. Several organizations have been formed to get the Bible to the people of the world. Caring Christians and churches provide money to groups like the American Bible Society and the Wycliffe Bible Translators. Hundreds of faithful people work at the task of translating the Bible into the language of every race and tribe in the world. They usually begin with the Gospel of John. The Bible's most precious promise can now be read by most of the people of the world in their own **tongue**. Have you memorized John 3:16?

You've read about the brave men who died to get the Bible translated into English. Every time the Bible is handed to a man or woman or boy or girl to read in his own language there's another story that goes with it. You may want to read about some of the brave people who suffered to carry out the command that Jesus left with His followers.

Read about William Carey who gave the Bible to India in 38 languages by his own hard work and determination.

A man named Morrison spent 13 years in China translating the Bible into Chinese. Eli Smith worked to prepare an Arabic Bible for the Moslem world. Archdeacon Dennis, in central Africa, spent a lifetime translating the Bible. As he was taking his precious manuscript back to England to be printed for his people, the ship in which he was traveling was sunk by an enemy torpedo. His manuscript was later found on the shores of Wales, but his own life was lost.

WORDS TO KNOW

tongue (tung)— *the language of a group of people.*

66

Then someone must take the Bible to the people. In most cases, this has been the work of missionaries. The Bible has gone almost everywhere that people can go:

— into remote Chinese villages
— atop the mountains of Peru
— up the rivers into jungles
— onto Indian reservations
— to prisoners behind bars
— to the blind in Braille
— into space with astronauts

Thousands upon thousands of people have given time, talent, prayer, and gifts to keep the message going into all the world. What about you? Will you be one of these?

THE BIBLE'S OWN STORY
REVIEW

TERMS AND NAMES	DEFINITIONS AND DESCRIPTIONS
1. inspired; inspiration	Words, ideas, and teachings that come from God.
2. papyrus	An Egyptian plant from which writing material is made.
3. parchment	A writing material made from the skins of animals, usually sheep and goats.
4. vellum	A fine quality of parchment made from the skins of young animals.
5. scroll	A long sheet of writing material that is rolled around two rods.
6. scribe	Someone who writes for another person or copies scripture.
7. scriptorium	A place where many men worked at copying scripture.
8. Massoretes	Scribes trained to copy the Old Testament scriptures accurately.
9. manuscript	Anything written by hand.
10. Essenes	A group of Jews dedicated to copying the Old Testament scriptures; lived near the Dead Sea; hid scrolls in caves.
11. Dead Sea Scrolls	Copies of Old Testament scriptures found in caves at Qumran near the Dead Sea.
12. Qumran	A small community near the Dead Sea where Essenes copied scriptures.
13. The Shrine of the Book	A museum in Jerusalem where the Dead Sea Scrolls are displayed.
14. archaeologist	A person who looks for information about ancient people by uncovering the places where they lived.
15. tell (or tel)	A hill that has been occupied by one town built on the remains of another.
16. artifacts	Objects made by ancient peoples. When found today, they give information about the people who made and used them.
17. sherds	Pieces of pottery. Some give valuable information about the people who made them.

TERMS AND NAMES	DEFINITIONS AND DESCRIPTIONS
18. codex	A manuscript put together in sheets and sewn together on the side.
19. canon	A list of books thought to be inspired by God.
*20. Apocrypha	The books left out of the Old Testament Canon because they were not considered to be inspired by God.
21. Jerome	Translated the Scriptures from Greek and Hebrew into Latin.
*22. Latin Vulgate	Jerome's translation of the Bible into Latin. The official Bible of the Church for many years.
23. Dark Ages	Period between A.D. 500 and 1000 when the Scriptures would have been lost if the monks had not protected them.
24. monks	Men who wanted to serve God and went to live in monasteries away from towns. Some of them gave their lives to the copying of the Scriptures.
25. monasteries	Places far away from towns where men could live who wanted to serve God only.
26. illuminations	Copies of the Scriptures that were decorated with pictures and designs.
*27. Septuagint	The Greek translation of the Old Testament. First translation into a language other than the original Hebrew.
28. paraphrase	Scripture that has been said in a different way from the original but has kept the original meaning.
*29. John Wycliffe	Translated the New Testament and most of the Old Testament into English.
30. Johann Gutenberg	Invented the printing press with movable type. Printed the Bible first.
*31. William Tyndale	Translated the New Testament from Greek to English and had it printed so more people could have it to read. He was burned at the stake for his "crime."
*32. Miles Coverdale	Translated the whole Bible into English.
*33. Geneva Bible	First Bible divided into chapters and verses.
34. King James Version	Translated by a group of scholars in England in 1611. After several revisions, it has become the most popular Bible of all time.

*HIGH CLIMBERS

Step 5

Bible Study Helps

Bible Study Helps

The Bible was inspired by God. He wants it to help us live for Him. This means we must read it and study it all of our lives. You've taken several steps toward being a good Bible student. You're on the right path. Deciding to be a good Bible student is one of the best decisions you'll ever make.

We're blessed to live in a time like this. Many people have tried to make it easier for us to study the Bible. There are many kinds of helps for Bible students. Some of them are right in the Bible itself. We've already seen how the books are divided into chapters and verses. That makes it easy for us to find any scripture reference we want quickly and easily. But this is just the beginning of the helps for us.

Take a look at your Bible. Most Bibles today have study aids. Some are in the front; some are in the back; and some are all through the Bible. There are also whole books and sets of books to help the Bible student understand the Bible better. Here is a list of some of them:

- Concordances
- Marginal references
- Bible atlases
- Footnotes
- Page headings
- Chapter headings
- Commentaries
- Dictionaries of Bible terms
- Harmonies of the Gospels
- Chronologies
- Genealogies
- Outlines and summaries of books
- Pictures and diagrams

It won't be necessary to study how to use all of these. You'll gradually learn about them as you study your Bible over the years. There are some, however, that are so helpful that any Bible student should know how to use them. As you learn to study the Bible for yourself, you'll be able to listen better to Bible teachers.

When they teach about a scripture, you can look it up and read it yourself. You can know if the teacher is telling you what the Bible really says.

This is another important skill for you to learn. If you're ready to take another step, come on along. We will get started.

TO TAKE THIS STEP—
Learn how to skillfully use each Bible help.

HIGH CLIMBERS Do all the work marked for High Climbers.

THE CONCORDANCE
WHAT IS A CONCORDANCE?

Have you ever heard a scripture verse and wondered where it was in the Bible? Unless you've been a Bible student for a long time, you wouldn't know where to begin looking for it. That's why some people get discouraged about using the Bible. They decide the Bible is just too big and too hard for them to study. "Let the preachers and Sunday School teachers do the studying," they think. What a mistake! If they only knew about the concordance and how to use it, they wouldn't give up so easily.

A concordance is a type of reference, something you "refer" to for a certain kind of information. Many types of books are used for looking up information. You probably already know how to use these reference books:

Dictionary — for looking up words, meanings, spellings, pronunciations, etc.

Encyclopedia — for finding facts and information about many topics.

Telephone directory — for finding telephone numbers, addresses and the correct spelling of names.

Bible scholars have gone through the entire Bible and listed every word anyone might need. They have listed them in such a way that you and I can find any verse we want by looking it up in a concordance.

Some Bibles have a concordance in them, but a concordance can also be a whole book by itself.

HOW CAN A CONCORDANCE HELP YOU?

1. It can help you find where a certain verse of scripture is located in the Bible.
2. It can help you find what the Bible says about a certain subject, what Jesus says, or what the Old Testament or the New Testament writers say about it.
3. Some concordances give definitions of words.
4. Some concordances tell who Bible characters are.
5. Some concordances give pronunciations of names.

A LAMP UNTO MY FEET

Order my steps in thy word; and let not any iniquity have dominion over me. (Palm 119:133)

HOW IS A CONCORDANCE ARRANGED?

Study these instructions about concordances. Spend some time with the sample sections from concordances. Then get a Bible that has a concordance and practice, practice, practice.

1. If a Bible has a concordance, it is usually in the back.

2. A concordance has pages and pages of terms called *entries*. Entries are the important words from scripture verses. Some concordances also include the names of people and places. Entries are listed in alphabetical order. They might be in dark print and stick out into the margin a little.

3. The entry is followed by a list of the Bible verses that have this term in them. Small concordances list only the most familiar verses. In any concordance, the whole verse is not written out. Only the line with the term in it is printed in the list. We'll refer to this as the *verse line*. In most concordances only the first letter of the entry word is given in the verse line. It isn't necessary to include the whole word.

4. A *scripture reference* comes either before or after the verse line. To save space, the name of the book is abbreviated as short as possible. These references are listed in the same order as the books in the Bible.

5. If the entry is a verb, the concordance might give all the forms of the verb with it. If it is a noun, the plural form is included.

Scripture References ----------

Entry word ----

SCOFF —ED —S*

Verse lines	
how the impious s. at thee all the	Ps 74.22
and s. at the Rock of his salvation.	Deu 32.15
heard all this, and they s. at him.	Lk 16.14
but the rulers s. at him, saying,	23.35
Plural form — how the enemy s., and an impious	Ps 74.18

SCOFFER —S

but a s. does not listen to rebuke.	Pro 13.01
"S." is the name of the proud,	21.24
come to nought and the s. cease,	Is 29.20
sinners, nor sits in the seat of s.;	Ps 1.01
How long will s. delight in their	Pro 1.22
'Behold, you s., and wonder, and	Ac 13.41
that s. will come in the last days	2Pe 3.03
"In the last time there will be s.,	Jud .18

SCOFFING (n)

Beware lest wrath entice you into s.;	Job 36.18
will come in the last days with s.,	2Pe 3.03

Verb endings ----

SCORCH* —ED —ING

it was allowed to s. men with fire;	Rev 16.08
but when the sun rose they were s.;	Mt 13.06
and his speech is like a s. fire.	Pro 16.27
burden of the day and the s. heat.'	Mt 20.12
rises with its s. heat and withers	Jas 1.11
you did not s. or despise me, but	Gal 4.14
s. by men, and despised by the	Ps 22.06
like a harlot, because you s. hire.	Eze 16.31

SENTENCE	CONCORDANCE	SHIELD

Sentence, utterance, decision.
Jer 4:12 give s. ag. them
Dn 5:12 shewing hard s.
Lk 23:24 Pilate gave s.
2 Co 1:9 had s. of death

Separate, divide, part.
Nu 6:2 s. themselves unto
1 K 8:53 s. them to be thy
Mt 25:32 s. as a shepherd
Lk 6:22 they shall s. you
Ro 8:35 who shall s. from
39 nothing able to s. us

Seraphim, angels of high order.
Is 6:2 above stood the s.
6 one of s. having coal

Serpent, snake.
Gn 3:1 s. was more subtile
49:17 Dan. a s. by way
Ex 4:3 rod become a s.
Nu 21:8 make thee fiery s.
2 K 18:4 Hez. brake s.
Ps 58:4 like poison of a s.
Pr 23:32 biteth like a s.
Is 27:1 Lord shall punish s.
30:6 fiery flying s.
65:25 dust be s. meat
Jer 8:17 send s. among
Mic 7:17 lick dust like a s.
Mt 7:10 give him a s.?
10:16 wise as s.
23:33 ye s., how escape?
Mk 16:18 take up s., and
Lk 10:19 to tread on s.
Jn 3:14 as Moses lifted up s.
Jas 3:7 kind of s. tamed
Rev 12:9 old s., the devil

Servant, helper, slave.
Gn 9:25 a s. of s. shall he be
Ex 21:5 s. say, love mas.
Dt 5:15 thou wast a s.
Job 3:19 there s. is free
4:18 no trust in his s.
7:2 s. desireth shadow.
Ps 105:17 sold for a s.
116:16 truly I am thy s.
135:14 repent concerning his s.
Pr 11:29 fool shall be s.
22:7 borrower is s. to
Ec 10:7 s. on horses, princes
Is 53:11 s. justify many
Dn 6:20 Daniel, s. of living
Mal 1:6 s. honoureth master
Mt 10:25 s. be as Lord
25:21 good and faithful s.
Mk 9:35 be s. of all
Lk 12:47 s. which knew his
17:9 doth he thank s.?
Jn 8:34 is the s. of sin
12:26 there my s. be
13:16 s. not greater than his
15:15 call you not s. for the s.
Ac 6:17 s. of high God
Ro 6:17 were s. of sin
18 s. of righteousness
1 Co 7:21 called being a s.
Gal 4:7 no more s. but a son
Ph 2:7 took form of a s.

Serve, obey, minister, assist.
Gn 15:13 s. them 400 yrs.
25:23 elder s. younger
29:18 s. 7 years for Rachel
Ex 1:13 made s. with rigour
4:23 son go, that may s.
Dt 6:13 fear Lord and s.
1 Ch 28:9 s. with perfect
Ps 72:11 all nations s. him
Jer 5:19 shall s. strangers
Zeph 3:9 s. him with one
Mt 6:24 no man can s. two
Lk 10:40 me to s. alone
Jn 12:26 if any s. me, let
Ro 6:6 should not s. sin
7:25 myself s. law of God
Gal 5:13 by love s. one ano.
Col 3:24 ye s. Lord Christ
1 Th 1:9 to s. the true God
He 9:14 to s. the living God
Rev 7:15 s. day and night

Service, spiritual obedience.
Ex 12:26 mean you by this s.
1 Ch 29:5 consecrate his s.
Jn 16:2 think doeth God s.
Ro 12:1 your reasonable s.
Eph 6:6 with eye s. as men-p.
7 s. as to the Lord

Servile, befitting a servant.
Lv 23:7 shall do no s. work

Set, to place, assume position.
Dt 30:15 s. before you life
Job 33:5 s. thy words in ord.
Ps 16:8 s. Lord always bef.
91:14 s. his love upon me
101:3 s. no wicked thing
Pr 8:23 s. up from everlast.
Ec 7:14 God s. one against
Jer 21:8 s. before you way of
Eph 1:20 s. him at own right
He 2:7 s. him over works of

Settle, establish, fix.
1 K 8:13 s. place for thee
2 K 8:11 s. his countenance
Ps 65:10 thou s. furrows
119:89 thy word is s.
Pr 8:25 bef. mts. were s.
Jer 48:11 Moab s. on lees
Zeph 1:12 are s. on lees
Col 1:23 in faith, s.

Seventy, seven times ten.
Gn 4:24 Lamech s. and sev.
Ex 1:5 of Jacob s. souls
24:1 Aaron and s. elders
Dn 9:24 s. weeks determined
Mt 18:22 s. times seven
Lk 10:1 appt'd other s.
17 s. returned with joy

Sever, separate, distinguish.
Ex 8:22 s. in that day
Lv 20:26 s. you from peo.
Mt 13:49 s. wicked from

Severity, extreme strictness.
Ro 11:22 goodness and s. of

Sew, join with stitches.
Gn 3:7 s. fig leaves
Job 16:15 s. sackcloth upon
Ec 3:7 time rend, time to s.
Mk 2:21 s. new cloth on

Shade, protection, cover.
Ps 121:5 Lord is thy s. upon

Shadow, shelter, security.
Job 7:2 earnestly desireth s.
Ps 17:8 hide me under s. of
91:1 under s. of Almighty
144:4 his days are as a s.
Cant 2:17 and s. flee away
Is 25:4 thou hast been a s.
32:2 of great rock in weary
Jer 6:4 s. of evening stretched
Lam 4:20 under his s. ye live
Ac 5:15 s. of Peter might
Col 2:17 s. of things to come
He 8:5 s. of heavenly things
Jas 1:17 with whom is no s.

Shaft, stem, stalk.
Ex 25:31 s. and branches
Is 49:2 me a polished s.

Shake, move rapidly, tremble.
Job 4:14 made bones to s.
Ps 29:8 Lord s. wilderness
Is 2:19 ariseth to s. earth
24:18 foundations of earth do
Ezk 38:20 all men s. at my
Hag 2:7 I will s. all nations
Mt 10:14 s. off the dust of
28:4 the keepers did s.
Lk 6:48 and could not s. it
He 12:26 s. not earth only

Shame, dishonor, deride.
Ps 4:2 turn my glory into s.
40:14 put to s. with me evil
Pr 11:2 then cometh s.
Is 54:4 shalt not be put to s.
Jer 51:51 s. hath covered our
Ezk 16:52 bear thine own s.
Zeph 3:5 unjust know. no s.

Ac 5:41 worthy to suffer s.
1 Co 6:5 speak of your s.
He 6:6 put him to open s.

Shape, form, figure.
Lk 3:22 in bodily s., like
12:22 despising the s.
Jn 5:37 voice, nor seen s.

Sharp, keen, sarcastic.
Ps 52:2 tongue like s. razor
Pr 5:4 s. as a two-edged
Is 41:15 thee s. instrument
Ac 15:39 contention was so s.

Shearer, one who shears sheep.
1 S 25:7 thou hast s.
Is 53:7 sheep before s.
Ac 8:32 lamb before s.

Sheath, case for sword.
1 S 17:51 Dav. drew out of s.
Jn 18:11 put sword into s.

Sheaves, bundles of grain.
Gn 37:7 binding s. in field
Ru 2:7 glean among s.
Ps 126:6 come bringing s.
Mic 4:12 gather as s.

Shed, cause to flow, diffuse.
Mt 26:28 s. for many for
Ac 2:33 Holy Ghost hath s.
Ro 5:5 love of God, s.
Tit 3:6 s. on us abundantly

Sheep, figuratively, people of God. Christians.
Gn 4:2 Abel was keeper of s.
Nu 27:17 as s. which have
Ps 8:7 all s. and oxen
44:22 counted as s. for
49:14 like s. are laid in grave
79:13 s. of thy pasture
95:7 s. of his hand
Is 53:6 like s. are gone
Jer 23:1 past. scatter s.
Ezk 34:6 My s. wander
Zec 13:7 s. be scattered
Mt 7:15 in s. clothing
10:6 lost s. of house of Isr.
12:12 man better than s.
18:13 rejoiceth more of that s.
25:33 s. on right hand
Jn 10:3 s. hear his voice
7 I am door of the s.
15 lay down my life for s.
21:16 to Peter, feed my s.
He 13:20 great Shepherd of s.
1 P 2:25 as s. going astray

Sheet, broad piece of cloth.
Jg 14:12 give you 30 s.
Ac 10:11 descending as a s.

Shelter, refuge, retreat.
Job 24:8 rock for want s.
Ps 61:3 been s. to me

Shepherd, keeper of sheep.
Gn 46:34 s. abom. to Egypt
49:24 s., stone of Israel
Ps 23:1 Lord is my s.
80:1 O S. of Israel
Is 40:11 feed flock like s.
Jer 23:4 set up s. over
50:6 s. caused to go astray
51:23 break s. and flock
Ezk 34:8 search for flock
23 one s. over them
Zec 11:16 raise up s. in the
17 woe to the idol s.
Lk 2:8 in same country s.
20 s. returned praising God
Jn 10:14 I am the good s.
He 13:20 Jesus that great s.
1 P 2:25 returned unto s.
5:4 chief s. shall appear

Shield, defense, protection.
Gn 15:1 I am thy s.
2 S 22:36 s. of salvation
Ps 33:20 Lord in our s.
84:11 God sun and s.
91:4 his truth shall be thy s.
Pr 30:5 s. to them that
Eph 6:16 taking s. of faith

THE NEW ANALYTICAL BIBLE
King James Version
John A. Dickson Publishing Co.

HOW DO YOU FIND A CERTAIN VERSE?

If you know a verse, or even part of it, but you don't know where it is in the Bible, you can find it easily with a concordance. Here's how to do it:

1. Decide which words in the verse are the *key words*. These are the most important words.
2. Look up one of the key words in the concordance. When you find that entry, read through the list of verse lines below it. You will probably come to the one you are wanting. What is the scripture reference?
3. Find the reference in the Bible and read the whole verse. If it's not the one you wanted, look up another of the key words. You may have to do this several times until you find the right one.
4. All concordances are not alike. Some have many more entry words than others. Suppose you don't find your key word listed in the concordance. Then try to think of another key word from the part of the verse that you know. See if it's listed in the concordance.

    Remember, some words appear so many times in the Bible that the list would be too long to help you.

A VERSE FOR PRACTICE

Where is this verse in the Bible?

> They who wait for the <u>Lord</u> shall <u>renew</u> their <u>strength</u>; they shall mount up with <u>wings</u> like <u>eagles</u>, they shall <u>run</u> and not be <u>weary</u>, <u>they</u> shall <u>walk</u> and not <u>faint</u>.

1. Decide on the key words. These have been underlined in the verse above.
2. Look up the key words one by one until you find the one you want. Here is what you would have found in one Bible concordance. Of course, the second key word would give you the reference. You would not have needed to look for others.

Lord .... word listed; this reference not given
* renew ...... yes; reference is given Is. 40:31
   wings .... word listed; this reference not given
* eagle .... yes; reference is given
* run .... yes; reference is given
   strength ... word listed; this reference not given
   weary ...... word listed; this reference not given
   walk .... word listed; this reference not given
   faint .... word listed; this reference not given
   they .... word not listed

WHAT DOES THE BIBLE SAY ABOUT THIS SUBJECT?

Have you ever wondered what God would say about something if you could ask Him? He has given us a way to find out. The Bible is His Word. In it He has told us who He is and how much He loves us. We can learn from the Bible what God says about the things that are right and wrong to do. It tells us what pleases Him. And yet, in all those books and chapters and verses, how will you know where to look? This is another time when the concordance can be your helper. We're going to look at a situation which could actually happen.

Suppose, in your Sunday School class last week, your friends began to discuss the subject of "honesty." Everyone seemed to have a different idea about what is right and wrong to do. Finally, your teacher suggested that each of you find out what *God* has to say about honesty. What a challenge! How will you find out? Will you ask someone else? He might possibly know a few places to look in the Bible. If you take your Bible and flip the pages something might catch your eye about honesty. But, then, you might never find what you really want to know.

Here's what you should do. Get a Bible with a concordance in the back. Look up the word *honesty*. If you don't find that word, try the word *honest*. If you find either of them, read all the verse lines. Write down the scripture references. Then start looking them up in the Bible, one by one. Don't stop after reading the first verse you looked up. Read the verses given before and after it as well. You might find that a whole chapter deals with that subject. After you have read each reference, stop and think about what you have read. Write down what you think God has said to you in that scripture.

Suppose your concordance doesn't have the word *honest* or *honesty*. Then you should look for related topics. These are subjects that mean the same or almost the same as the original one. For example, you might find some good references under *truth* or *lying* or *integrity*.

Since you know something about the books of the Bible, you'll be able to find out many things from your concordance. You could limit your search to learn only what Jesus said about it. To do this, use only the references from the Gospels. Or, if you want to know what Paul said, use only the letters written by Paul. Or, if you want to know what the Old Testament said, use only Old Testament references. Do you see how your skills are beginning to work for you?

If you have a Bible that doesn't have a concordance, you can buy a separate concordance in a store where Bibles are sold. There are many kinds, from small paperbacks to huge, heavy ones.

MARGINAL REFERENCES

Have you ever seen a Bible with a little strip down the center or on one side of the page? The print in that little strip is very tiny and mysterious-looking. These strips are called by different names:

-marginal references -chain references

-column references -cross references

The first name is the one we'll use. We're going to take a look at marginal references. When you find out what they are and how to use them, they won't look mysterious to you any longer. You'll see what a help they can be to a good Bible student.

This sample page is taken from the book of I John. Find 3:11. Read verses 11 and 12. Now look at the center column. Slide your finger down the left side of it until you come to "3:11". Keep a finger on that reference in the column and write down all the references beside it. If you look up all those references you'll find other teachings about the same thing that is in this verse: I Jn. 1:5, 2:7; Jn. 13:34-35, 15:12; I Jn. 4:7, 11-12, 21; and II Jn. 5. Did you have trouble reading the references?

Look again at verse 12. It mentions Cain, who killed his brother. How quickly can you tell where to find that story in the Old Testament? Did you have to look in the many books of the Old Testament? Did you guess where it might be and turn there to check it out? You wouldn't need to look anywhere else but this page. Find the "3:12" in the column. It gives "Gen. 4:8." That's where the story is in the Old Testament. You can turn there and read it if you wish. Can you see how much a marginal reference can help you?

---

us, *e* eternal life.

26 I write this to you about those who would deceive you; 27 but the anointing which you received from him abides in you, and you have no need that any one should teach you; as his anointing teaches you about everything, and is true, and is no lie, just as it has taught you, abide in him.

28 And now, little children, abide in him, so that when he appears we may have confidence and not shrink from him in shame at his coming. 29 If you know that he is righteous, you may be sure that every one who does right is born of him.

3 See what love the Father has given us, that we should be called children of God; and so we

```
Jn 3.10: Mt
4.3; Mk 1.24:
Jn 12.31.
16.11
3.9: Mt 7.18:
13.37-38: 2
Cor 13.8: Jas
1.18: 1 Pet
1.23: 1 Jn
3.6; 5.18: 3
Jn 11
3.10: Jn 1 12:
11.52; Rom
8.16; 1 Jn 3.1-
2: Mt 13.38
3.11: 1 Jn
1.5; 2.7: Jn
13.34-35:
15.12: 1 Jn
4.7, 11-12, 21:
2 Jn 5
3.12: Gen 4.8:
Prov 29.10:
Jn 8 40-41:
Wisdom 2.12
3.13: Jn
15.18-19:
17.14
3.14: Jn 5.24:
13.35: 1 Jn
2.10
3.15: Mt 5.21-
22: Jn 8.44:
Rev 21.8
3.16: Jn 10.11:
13.1, 14:
15.13: Phil
2.17
```

nor he who does not love his brother.

11 For this is the message which you have heard from the beginning, that we should love one another. 12 and not be like Cain who was of the evil one and murdered his brother. And why did he murder him? Because his own deeds were evil and his brother's righteous. 13 Do not wonder, brethren, that the world hates you. 14 We know that we have passed out of death into life, because we love the brethren. He who does not love remains in death. 15 Any one who hates his brother is a murderer, and you know that no murderer has eternal life abiding in him. 16 By this we know love, that he laid down his life for us; and we ought to lay down our lives for the

REVISED STANDARD VERSION

Reference Edition with Concise Concordance

Thomas Nelson and Sons

In this Bible the reference column is on the side of the page. It's easy to find which references go with each verse. They're right beside it. There are tiny letters in front of some of the words. Find the same letters in the column under that verse number. Now you know exactly where to look in the Bible to find another scripture with this same meaning.

Find verse 8. Now find the 8 in the column at the end of it. Two references are given. What are they? Did you find I John 4:16 and I John 4:7? Since one of them is in this sample page, you can read it and see if it's like this one in meaning.

A LAMP UNTO MY FEET

And be not conformed to this world: but be ye transformed by the renewing of your mind, that ye may prove what is that good, and acceptable, and perfect, will of God. (Romans 12:2)

The Spirit of Error.
God Is Love.   No Fear In Love.

1 John 4, 5

3   and every spirit that ᵃdoes not confess Jesus is not from God; and this is the *spirit* of the ᵇantichrist, of which you have heard that it is coming, and ᶜnow it is already in the world.

4   You are from God, ᵃlittle children, and ᵇhave overcome them; because ᶜgreater is He who is in you than ᵈhe who is in the world.

5   ᵃThey are from the world; therefore they speak *as* from the world, and the world listens to them.

6   ᵃWe are from God; ᵇhe who knows God listens to us; ᶜhe who is not from God does not listen to us. By this we know ᵈthe spirit of truth and ᵉthe spirit of error.

7   ᵃBeloved, let us ᵇlove one another, for love is from God; and ᶜevery one who loves is ¹ᵈborn of God and ᵉknows God.

8   The one who does not love does not know God, for ᵃGod is love.

9   By this the love of God was manifested ¹ᵃin us, that ᵇGod has sent His ²only begotten Son into the world so that we might live through Him.

10   In this is love, ᵃnot that we ¹loved God, but that ᵇHe loved us and sent His Son *to be* ᶜthe propitiation for our sins.

11   ᵃBeloved, if God so loved us, ᵇwe also ought to love one another.

12   ᵃNo one has beheld God at any time; if we love one another, God abides in us, and His ᵇlove is perfected in us.

13   ᵃBy this we know that we abide in Him and He in us, because He has given us of His Spirit.

3 ᵃ2 John 7; 1 John 2:22 ᵇ1 John 2:22; 2:18 ᶜ1 John 2:18; 2 Thess. 2:3-7

4 ᵃ1 John 2:1 ᵇ1 John 2:13 ᶜ1 John 3:20; 2 Kin. 2:16; Rom. 8:31 ᵈJohn 12:31

5 ᵃJohn 15:19; 17:14, 16

6 ᵃ1 John 4:4; John 8:23 ᵇJohn 8:47; 10:3ff.; 18:37 ᶜ1 Cor. 14:37 ᵈJohn 14:17 ᵉ1 Tim. 4:1

7 ¹Or, *begotten* ᵃ1 John 2:7 ᵇ1 John 3:11 ᶜ1 John 5:1 ᵈ1 John 2:29 ᵉ1 John 2:3; 1 Cor. 8:3

8 ᵃ1 John 4:16; 1 John 4:7

9 ¹Or, *in our case* ²Or, *unique, only one of His kind* ᵃ1 John 4:16; John 9:3 ᵇJohn 3:16f.; 1 John 4:10; 5:11

10 ¹Some mss. read, *had loved* ᵃRom. 5:8, 10; 1 John 4:19 ᵇJohn 3:16f.; 1 John 4:9; 5:11 ᶜ1 John 2:2

11 ᵃ1 John 2:7 ᵇ1 John 4:7

12 ᵃJohn 1:18; 1 Tim. 6:16; 1 John 4:20 ᵇ1 John 2:5; 4:17f.

13 ᵃ1 John 3:24; Rom. 8:9

NEW AMERICAN STANDARD
World Publishing

doeth not righteousness is not of God, neither he that loveth not his brother.
Ch. 2.29; 4.8.

11 For this is the message that ye heard from the beginning, that we should love one another.
Ch. 1.5; 4.7,21; Jo. 13.34; 15.12.

12 Not as Cain, *who* was of that wicked [of the evil] one, and slew his brother. And wherefore slew he him? Because his own works were evil, and his brother's righteous.
Ge. 4.4,8; He. 11.4; Jude 11.

13 Marvel not, my brethren, if the world hate you.
Jo. 15.18,19; 17.14; 2 Ti. 3.12.

14 We know that we have passed from death unto life, because we love the brethren. He that loveth not *his* brother [omit his brother] abideth in death.
Ch. 2.9-11.

15 Whosoever hateth his brother is a murderer: and ye know that no murderer hath eternal life abiding in him.
Ma. 5.21,22. Ga. 5.21; Re. 21.8.

CHAPTER 4.
1 He warneth them not to believe all teachers who boast of the Spirit, but to try the spirits, & c.

BELOVED, believe not every spirit, but try the spirits whether they are of God: because many false prophets are gone out into the world.
Ch. 2.18; Ma. 24.4,5,24; 1 Th. 5.21; 2 Pe. 2.1; Re. 2.2.

2 Hereby know ye the Spirit of God: Every spirit that confesseth that Jē'-ṡŭs Chrīst is come in the flesh is of God:
Ch. 5.1; 1 Co. 12.3.

3 And every spirit that confesseth not that Jē-ṡŭs Chrīst is come in the flesh [R. V. omits Christ ís come in the flesh] is not of God: and this is that *spirit* of ăn'-tǐ-chrīst, whereof ye have heard that it should come; and even now already is it in the world.
Ch. 2.18,22; 2 Th. 2.7; 2 Jo. 7.

4 Ye are of God, little children, and have overcome them: because greater is he that is in you, that he that is in the world.
Ch. 5.4; Jo. 16.11; 1 Co. 2.12; Ep. 2.2; 6.12.

NEW ANALYTICAL BIBLE

In this Bible sample there is no column, but there are references. Can you find them? You don't need to follow numbers and letters to the column. The references about each verse are printed below the verse.

This sample is from I John 3 and 4. Look for 4:4 and read it. How many references are given? Can you read all of them?

Ch. 5.4 — Read *Chapter five (of this book), verse four.*

Jo. 16.11 — Read *John sixteen, verse eleven.*

I Co. 2.12 — Read *First Corinthians two, verse twelve.*

Ep. 2.2; 6.12 — Read *Ephesians two, verse two; and six, twelve.*

HOW DO MARGINAL REFERENCES HELP?

If you're doing a study of a certain subject, such as "love," you can read one scripture about it and then look up the references and find more. When you get to those scriptures, there may be references with them. Follow up those references to see what else the scriptures say about the subject. You can keep doing this until you have read most of what the Bible has said about it.

The Bible stories are filled with quotations from Old Testament writers or references to events in Hebrew history. Events in the Old Testament are often background for what happened after Jesus came. It's easy to check the marginal references to see where these scriptures are.

Le'shem. A city in the north of Palestine (Josh. 19.47), also called Laish.

Le-tu'shim. Second son of Dedan, Abraham's grandson by Keturah (Gen. 25.3). From him this tribe descended. Probably settled in Arabia.

Le-um'mim (nations). The last of the sons of Dedan (Gen. 25.3), the tribe descended from him indicated by the plural of the word. Settled in Arabia.

Le'vi (adhesion). 1. Third son of Jacob by Leah (Gen. 29.34). His part in the crime at Shechem (Gen. 34.25-31) and Jacob's dying reference to it (49.7). His three sons were Gershon or Gershom, Kohath, Merari (Gen. 46.11). He died in Egypt at the age of 137 (Ex. 6.16). See LEVITES.

     2. Son of Melchi and father of Matthat, ancestor of Jesus (Lu. 3.24).

     3. Son of Simeon and father of another Matthat, an ancestor of Jesus (Lu. 3.29).

     4. The first name of the apostle Matthew

6.18; Neh. 13.5). Luke notes that Jesus entered upon His public ministry, inaugurated by baptism, when thirty years of age (3.23). See pp. 160,216.

Le-vit'i-cus (relating to the Levites).

Introductory statement. See pg. 125.

Chart outline of the book. Pg. 126.

Outline of contents in detail. Pp. 160, 161.

The Sacrificial Idea. Pg. 161.

Sacredness of Institutions. Pg. 162.

Sacred Seasons. Pp.162-164.

New Testament References to Leviticus. Pg. 164.

The Tabernacle. Pp. 165,166.

Lib'er-tines (freedmen). The word occurs in Acts 6.9. They were Jews made captive by the Romans under Pompey and were set free. They built a synagogue at Je-

NEW ANALYTICAL BIBLE

OTHER BIBLE STUDY HELPS

BIBLE DICTIONARIES

There are many kinds of books available to the Bible student. One includes special dictionaries. Sometimes you can find a Bible with a dictionary in it. Or you can buy a special one as you get to be more and more interested in studying the Bible.

OUTLINES AND SUMMARIES

Someday you may want to buy a new Bible. When you do, there are some helpful things to look for. A good study Bible will often have outlines and summaries with the books of the Bible. This may not seem important now, but these can become a valuable tool for you later. Spend some time looking through the Bible before you buy it. Make sure you have the one that can help you be a better Bible student.

OUTLINE OF THE FIRST EPISTLE OF JOHN

I. The Divine Light, 1.5—2.28.
In the opening verses John states the object of the epistle, 1.1-4.
   1. Fellowship with God. To have such we must walk in the light.
   2. We walk in the light by keeping His commandments.

II. Marks of the New Birth, 2.29—5.5.
   1. Righteous conduct the result of the new birth, as unrighteousness indicates that it has not taken place.
   2. The true distinguished from the false by the regenerated man.

   3. The denial of the Incarnation not compatible with the new birth.
   4. The new birth exhibited in brotherly love. That God is love is the prevailing note of the epistle.

III. God in the Incarnate Christ, 5.6-21.
Fellowship with God made possible only through the incarnate Christ.
   1. The true believer has the witness in himself, in his own spiritual life.
   2. When the life is under the rulership of sin and not under the sovereignty of Christ.
   3. Fellowship with God grounded in the belief in the Incarnate Son.

NEW ANALYTICAL BIBLE

Step 6

Bible Lands

Bible Lands

The stories of the Bible tell about real events that happened to real people. As a Bible student, you will want to know the real places where they happened. It will help you understand the stories much better.

The part of the world where the events in the Bible took place is far away from our country. You probably haven't studied it before. That's why we're going to take this step on the pathway to Bible skills. You'll be looking at maps of the Bible lands to see what they are like. You'll learn about cities, rivers, mountains, and deserts. After this study, when you hear a Bible story, you'll know where that place is on the map.

TO TAKE THIS STEP —

Learn to locate each place in this section that is in boldface type. Be able to use a Bible atlas to find these places on maps.

HIGH CLIMBERS

Label and color a map of the O.T. World. Do the High Climbers Page.

THE OLD TESTAMENT WORLD

The Old Testament events took place in a very small area. In fact, it's less than half the size of the United States. About one-third of it is desert. Look at the map of the Old Testament World. See where its boundaries were. Now, get ready. We're going to take a "fingerwalk" around this part of the world and pretend we're living in the days of Old Testament history.

The right side of a map is usually the east. Begin in the east. Find the top of the **Persian Gulf.** Put your finger on it. The name for this region is **Mesopotamia** (MES ō pō TĀ mi uh). That word means "land between rivers." The rivers are the **Tigris** (TĪ gris), on the east, and the **Euphrates** (ū FRĀ tēz), on the west. Mesopotamia was a good valley for growing many kinds of crops. It was 600 miles long — from the Persian Gulf in the south to the Taurus Mountains in the north. This region was very important in Bible history.

While you're in Mesopotamia, take a look at some of these important places.

Babylonia — This was a nation located in Mesopotamia. It came to great power during the last part of the history of the Southern Kingdom, Judah. The Babylonians destroyed Jerusalem and took many Hebrew people into captivity.

An older name for Babylonia is **Chaldea.** Do you remember Abraham? He came from Ur of the Chaldees. God called him to leave there and begin a new life in another place.

Nineveh — This city grew to be very large and powerful. It was the capital of the Assyrian Empire. Can you find this city and Assyria to the east of the Tigris River?

Haran — This city was in the northern part of the Mesopotamian Valley. Abraham lived there for awhile after he left Ur. Later, his son Isaac married a girl from Haran. Then their son Jacob lived in Haran for many years.

Follow the valley north and then turn left toward the west. You will come to the land of **Asia Minor.** This was the home of the ancient Hittites (HIT īts). Today it is known as the country of Turkey.

Now turn southeastward. You will come to **Syria.** On the left (west) of Syria is a large sea. What is its name? On the right (east) is a desert. Syria has two mountain ranges. The most important are the **Lebanon Mountains.** There were some important cities in this region. **Damascus** was the chief city. It's still the capital of

Syria today. **Tyre** (tīr) and **Sidon** (SĪ don) were busy trade centers on the coast.

Move your finger toward the south. You should now be in **Palestine** (PAL es tīn). Here's where most of the history of the Bible took place. In fact, it's so important that we'll come back to it and study it better.

Egypt is on the continent of Africa. It's separated from Asia by the **Red Sea**. Because of the **Nile River**, Egypt was one of the first places where human beings lived. It was already a powerful nation long before Abraham was born. Egypt's history was tied to Hebrew history in many Bible stories. The Nile River was what made Egypt great. As you get away from the river and its valley, you find only dry desert.

Between Egypt and Arabia is a small triangle of land. Can you find it at the top of the Red Sea? It's called the **Sinai** (SĪ ni) **Peninsula**. It's mostly wilderness. And yet, it was home to the Hebrews for over 40 years when they left Egypt. Can you find **Mt. Sinai** at the lower end of it? This is where God gave the Ten Commandments and much of the Law to Moses and the Israelites.

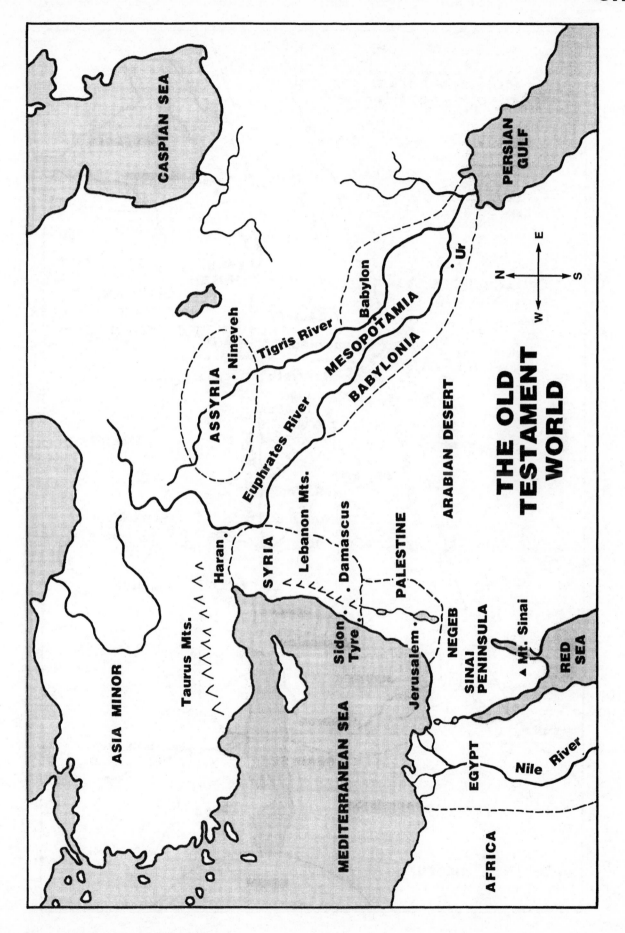

THE OLD TESTAMENT WORLD

CASPIAN SEA

PERSIAN GULF

ASSYRIA · Nineveh

Tigris River

Babylon

MESOPOTAMIA

· Ur

BABYLONIA

Euphrates River

ARABIAN DESERT

Haran ·

SYRIA

Lebanon Mts.

· Damascus

PALESTINE

Taurus Mts.

Sidon ·
Tyre ·

Jerusalem ·

NEGEB

ASIA MINOR

MEDITERRANEAN SEA

SINAI
PENINSULA

▲ Mt. Sinai

RED
SEA

EGYPT

Nile River

AFRICA

N   E
W   S

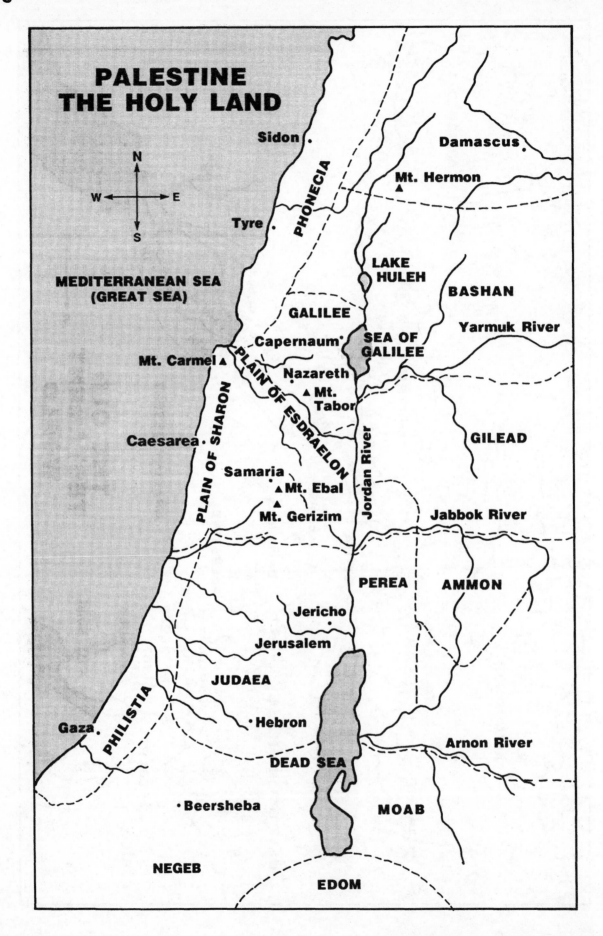

PALESTINE THE HOLY LAND

Sidon

Damascus

PHONECIA

Mt. Hermon ▲

Tyre

MEDITERRANEAN SEA (GREAT SEA)

LAKE HULEH

BASHAN

GALILEE

Yarmuk River

Capernaum

SEA OF GALILEE

Mt. Carmel ▲

PLAIN OF SHARON

PLAIN OF ESDRAELON

Nazareth

▲ Mt. Tabor

Caesarea

Jordan River

GILEAD

Samaria

▲ Mt. Ebal

▲ Mt. Gerizim

Jabbok River

PEREA

AMMON

Jericho

Jerusalem

JUDAEA

Gaza

PHILISTIA

Hebron

DEAD SEA

Arnon River

Beersheba

MOAB

NEGEB

EDOM

PALESTINE

Now we'll study the map of Palestine more carefully. This small land could be called the center of the whole world. It's where many important events took place. In fact, it's still the most important place in the whole world. As you study the Bible more, you'll come to see why this is true.

This small piece of land has been called by many names throughout its history. Its earliest name was **Canaan** (KĀ nan). The Canaanites lived there before the Hebrews arrived. Palestine is the name by which it was called in later years. The word **Palestine** means "the land of the Philistines." The Philistines (FIL i stēnz) lived on the southwest coast of Palestine. The Hebrews called this land the **Promised Land** because God had promised it to Abraham and his family in the covenant. Today it's called **Israel**, and its citizens are called Israelis. We'll use the name Palestine for our study because that's the name it's given in most Bible atlases.

Christians call it their Holy Land because it was where Jesus was born. He was the Messiah who had been promised in Hebrew prophecy. It was in this land that He lived and taught. He died here and was buried in a tomb in Jerusalem. But He rose from the tomb, and His tomb is empty today. After His death, the apostles preached in Jerusalem and in Samaria and all parts of Palestine. Many Jews became followers of Christ and were called Christians. The Church began in this land. There are hundreds of Christian churches in Israel today. Thousands of Christians from all over the world visit these holy places every year.

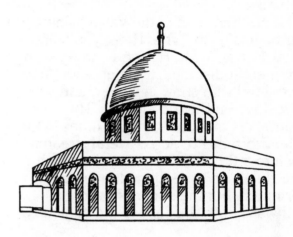

Many years after the time of Christ, the land was taken over by Moslems (MOZ lumz). These people from Arabia worship a leader named Mohammed (mō HAM ed). The Moslems held Palestine for many years. They call it a holy land just as the Jews do. They worship in buildings called **mosques** (mosks). Visitors to Israel can see Moslem mosques in many places. Many Arabs still live in Israel. They know the stories of the Old Testament characters, but they don't use our Bible. They have their own scriptures, called the Koran, (Kō RON) a collection of the writings of Mohammed.

This small country is somewhat set apart from the rest of the world. It has deserts on the south and east, and mountains on the north. The Mediterranean Sea is on the west. And yet, it has been crossed by travelers from everywhere in the world. It's located between Asia, Africa and Europe. It was often conquered by the armies of powerful nations around it. Men from all three continents met in the cities of this small country to trade with one another.

PHYSICAL FEATURES AND DIVISIONS

Jordan River Valley

Palestine is divided into two parts by a deep, wide valley. This valley is like a deep cut running from north to south through the length of the land. Three lakes are in this valley. The Jordan River connects them all.

The northern end of the valley, where the river begins, is in Syria. Here, you'll find **Mount Hermon**. Mt. Hermon can be seen from a great distance. It's high enough to be covered with snow in winter, and some snow stays on the top all year. The mountain is mentioned many times in the Bible. From this region, several streams flow into a tiny lake named Lake Huleh. Lake Huleh isn't mentioned in the Bible very much, but the stream flowing southward from this lake is the beginning

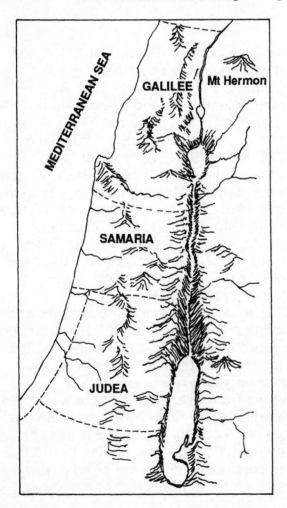

of the **Jordan River**. The river falls very steeply, creating many small waterfalls as it runs through the valley. It empties into the **Sea of Galilee**, a beautiful lake. (In the Bible, almost any body of water is called a sea.)

The Sea of Galilee is called by several names in the Bible:
— Lake of Gennesaret (ge NES a ret)
— Lake, or Sea, of Chinnereth (KIN uh reth)
— Sea of Tiberias (tī BI ri us)

It's about eight miles wide and 14 miles long. Many of the events in the life of Jesus took place on or around this lake. The Sea of Galilee and the region around it are about 680 feet below sea level (the level of the water in the ocean). It's shaped somewhat like a bowl, with low, rounded mountains rising near every side. Many fishermen make their living from the lake, but they must always beware of sudden storms which come upon it.

The Jordan River flows out of the Sea of Galilee through one of the deepest valleys in the world. The valley itself is only 65 miles long, but the river is so crooked that it measures 110 miles in length as it goes through the valley. The river is from 100 to 200 feet wide. Since it's at the bottom of the "cut," there are no cities along its banks and, during certain seasons every year, the river overflows its banks. It can't be used for watering crops or for transportation. No bridges were built across it until 1917, when a bridge was built near Jericho. Two rivers, the **Yarmuk** (yar MŌOK) and the **Jabbok** (JAB ok), flow into the Jordan from the east side. The map shows other smaller streams flowing into it, but these are wadis (WAH diz). A wadi is a stream that is dry except during periods of rainfall.

A much larger body of water is located at the southern end of the Jordan River. It catches the water from the Jordan and holds it because there is no other stream by which the water may leave. The hot sun continuously evaporates the water in this sea, leaving behind the minerals brought downstream by the Jordan River. This makes the sea so full of salt and chemicals that no plants or animals can live in it. Once it was called the Salt Sea, but today its name is the **Dead Sea**. It is 1,286 feet below sea level — the lowest place on earth.

Today, along its shores, there are beaches where people can go into the water. They can't actually swim, however, because the water is much too thick with salt. Most people just float and wade. Then they must go quickly to the clean, clear water of a shower and wash off the salt.

To the west of the Dead Sea is a large desert region called the **Negeb**. The only people who live here are the shepherds who come during the season when there is some grass.

A LAMP UNTO MY FEET

And Jesus increased in wisdom, and stature, and in favor with God and man. (Luke 2:52)

West of the Jordan

Since the Jordan Valley divides Palestine into two parts, we'll study each separately. First we'll look at the part on the west side and then we'll study the part on the east.

The western area has three kinds of geography. There's a plateau in the north, a highland in the middle, and a coastal plain in the south.

The plateau, itself, is divided into three sections. **Galilee**, the farthest north, is in the mountains. The Jordan River and the Sea of Galilee are on its eastern boundary, and it's separated from Samaria on the south by the Plain of Esdraelon. Jesus grew up in this northern region of Galilee. Can you find his boyhood town of **Nazareth** on your map? Other Galilean cities mentioned in the Bible are **Cana** (KĀ nuh), **Capernaum** (kuh PER nā uhm), and **Bethsaida** (Beth SĀ i duh). Look for these cities, too. Many of the miracles of

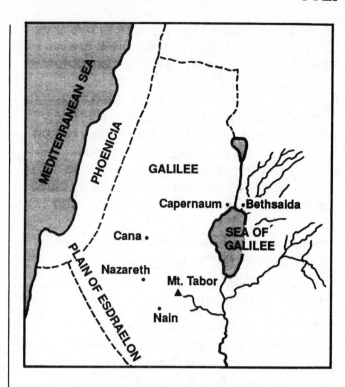

Jesus were performed at these towns. Some of the disciples fished in the Sea of Galilee. It was here that Jesus calmed the storm. And once He walked on the water.

Samaria (suh MĀ ri uh) is the middle section. On the east is the **Jordan**, and on the west is the **Plain of Sharon**. This area is a good place to live. It was the homeland of Abraham and his sons and grandsons. Later, some of the Israelite tribes settled here. Its main city is also

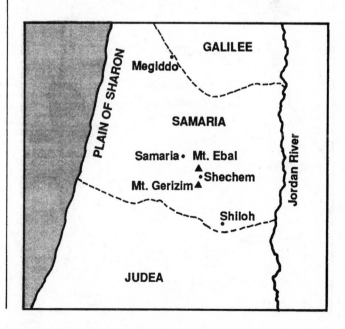

named Samaria. Other places in this area which are mentioned in the Bible are **Shechem** (SHĒ kem), **Shiloh** (SHĪ lō), **Mt. Ebal** (Ē bahl), **Mt. Gerizim** (ge RĪ zim), and **Megiddo** (me GID ō).

Judea (joo DĒ uh), or Judah, is the southernmost section. Much of this region is rocky. And yet, it has some good pastures. It has been important in the history of the Jews. Some important cities are located in Judea. Find these on the map:

Jerusalem (ji ROO sah lem)
Bethlehem (BETH le hem)
Jericho (JER i kō)
Hebron (HĒ bron)
Beersheba (BĒ er SHĒ buh)

Northeast of **Jerusalem** is **Jericho**. Today, travelers to Jericho from Jerusalem take the same road that Jesus and the disciples walked many years ago. Of course, it's paved today, and most people go by car or bus. Jericho is one of the oldest cities in the world. Many Jerichos have been built on the same spot over the centuries. You may remember the one that was destroyed by the Israelites when they came into the Promised Land.

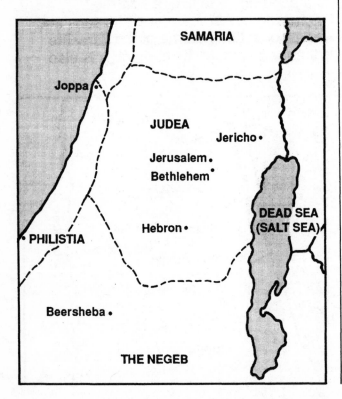

Bethlehem is about five miles south of Jerusalem. Of course, you know that Bethlehem is the city where Jesus was born. Today, there's a large old church built over the place where he was born, and visitors come from all over the world to see it. The bells in the church ring only one time a year — on the morning of Christmas Day. There are still shepherds keeping watch over sheep in the fields nearby, just as they were on the night when the angels appeared and told the Good News.

If you go farther south from Jerusalem, you'll come to **Hebron**. Hebron is where Abraham lived when he went to Canaan. When Sarah died, Abraham bought a cave at Hebron and buried her there. Today, there is a large church built over the tombs of Sarah and Abraham and several other Bible characters.

On your map, Beersheba is not actually in Judea. However, at times in the past, Judea was large and did take in this city. Beersheba is on the edge of the Negeb Desert. Abraham lived there for many years. According to the Bible, the wells he dug were the source of trouble several times. Beersheba is mentioned in many Old Testament stories.

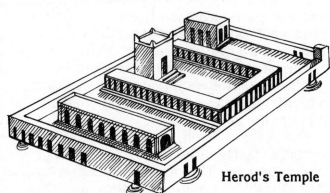

Herod's Temple

Jerusalem

While we're here in Judea, we should spend a little time in Jerusalem, one of the most exciting cities in the world. It's the most important city for the people of three religions: Jews, Moslems, and Christians. It has been the center of Bible history since King David chose it for his capital.

The Old City

It's still the center of Jewish worship. Three temples have been built on almost the same spot in Jerusalem. The last one was the Temple built by Herod the Great. Jesus and His friends worshiped in Herod's Temple.

The city today is really like two cities. Old Jerusalem looks like a city from the Middle Ages. It covers an area of about one square mile and has a high, stone wall surrounding it on all sides. The wall has eight gates, but one of them has been closed with bricks for many years. Behind the walls are narrow, winding streets. Only one corner of the city has streets where cars come and go; the other parts are not suited for traffic. Some streets have steps leading from one level to another. Arches cover some of the streets and make them rather dark. Tiny shops line each side of the street. The shops are so small that shopkeepers don't have room inside for showing their products. Therefore, they hang much of it outside on hooks along the walls and over the doorways.

It's easy to see that the Old City is shared by many religions. People in all kinds of costumes can be seen going and coming along the little streets. The city has four parts, called "quarters." Each quarter is used by a different culture: Jews, Moslems, Christians, and Armenians. Since donkeys are used to bring in loads of goods for the shops, the streets are always crowded with people and animals.

Outside the Old City's walls, on three sides, is a large, new Jerusalem with wide streets and modern buildings. On the east side is the Mount of Olives.

Many Bible scholars believe that events of endtime prophecy will take place in this wonderful city.

Phoenicia and Philistia

Between the highlands and the Mediterranean Sea lies a coastal plain. This is only a mile or two wide on the north. But it widens to about 30 miles on the south. In the north, between Galilee and the Mediterranean Sea, is the region called **Phoenicia** (fi NISH uh). The early Phoenicians who lived here were greatly interested in the sea. They were famous for ship building, sailing, and trading. The cities of Tyre and Sidon are often mentioned in the Bible stories. Skilled workers from these cities helped Solomon build ships and buildings.

Just south of Phoenicia, the coastline sticks out into the sea. This is **Mount Carmel** (KAR mel). Below this point is the Plain of Sharon, a land of gardens and fruit trees. To the south of this plain is **Philistia**. The Philistines (fi LIS tēnz) were almost always enemies of the Hebrews. The Bible has many stories about the wars between them. Some of the important cities were **Gaza** (GAH zuh), **Ashkelon** (ASH ke lon), and **Joppa** (JAH pah).

East of the Jordan

Control of the land east of the Jordan Valley has changed hands often. Therefore, the names of the divisions and the boundaries on a map will depend upon which period of history is being shown on that map. This is true, of course, of all the countries of the Bible world.

The region between Mt. Hermon and the Yarmuk River was known as **Bashan** (BĀ shan) in Old Testament times. It's high and rocky, but some of it is good for crops.

Between the Yarmuk and the Jabbok is an area known as **Gilead** (GIL ē ad). During the ministry of Jesus it was known as **Perea** (pe RĒ ah).

South of the Jabbok, east of Perea, is **Ammon** (AM on). It runs south to the Arnon River. To the east of the Dead Sea, and south of the Arnon, is **Moab** (MŌ ab). South of the Dead Sea is **Edom** (Ē dom). The people of these regions were called the Ammonites, the Moabites, and the Edomites. They are in many Bible stories.

THE BIBLE ATLAS

A Bible atlas is another helpful reference for a Bible student. It can save a great deal of time and give you the information you need. If you use it, you will understand what you read in the Bible much better. Many Bibles have maps in the back. Or

you can buy a book that is called a Bible atlas which will give many more maps and much more information about the Bible world.

READING A MAP INDEX

Finding a place on a map would be almost impossible if there were no index to the maps. A map index isn't like the index in a book. That's why we're going to learn what it is and how to use it. You won't be able to use Bible maps with confidence unless you know this skill.

In an atlas with many maps, the maps are identified in some way. They may be numbered with regular numbers (1, 2, 3, 4. . .) or Roman numerals (I, II, III, IV. . .). Sometimes these are called **map numbers**, and sometimes they are called **plate numbers**. Look for these in your own atlas. They're usually printed at the top of the page on each map. The map index is usually located before or after the set of maps. It lists the names of almost anything you might want to find on the map. Regions, cities, mountains, rivers, seas, and deserts are all listed in alphabetical order. Some give a definition or short description of that place. Each one has some numerals, letters, and punctuation marks.

Kefr-Bir'im..B3 XIV, XV, XVI	Laranda............B5 XX	*Madon, 139*
Keilah...E2 III; E3 VI, VII, VIII, IX, X	Larissa...B1 XIII; D10 XIX; B3 XX	Maeander, riv...B2 XI, XIII; B4 XX
Keilah, 185	Larsa.............C6 III, XI	Magan.............D3 III
Kelishin Pass.........B6 XI	*Larsa, 323*	Magdala (Tarichaea) .C3 XIV, XV, XVI
Kenites ..B6 V; F3 VI, VII, VIII, IX, X	Lase Matala.........B3 XX	*Magdala, 374, 380*
Kephar Uzziel, 358	*Lasha, 52*	Magharah, mtn.........D5 V
Kerak, Khirbet .....D2 XXI	Lauriacum ....B9 XIX	Magnesia. . .B2 XI, XIII; B4 XX
Kerkha, riv..........C6 XI	Laxaries.........B12 XII	*Magnesia, 467*
Kermanshah..........C6 III	Lebanon............C3 XXI	Magog.............B6 IV
Keykavus Kaleh......B4 III	Lebanon, mtn..A2 I; C4 XI; A4 XIV, XV, XVI; C6 XX	Mahanaim. .D4 VI, VII, IX, X
Kezib, 90	*Lebanon, min., 330*	*Mahanaim, 84, 85, 204–06*
Khabur, riv........B5 III, XI	Lebonah.. D3 VI, VII, VIII, IX, X, XIV, XV, XVI	*Mahaneh-dan, 163, 167*
Khaduttu...........B4 XI	*Lebonah (el Lebban), 365*	Mahra.. . ...D7 IV
Khafajeh........C5 III, XXI	Lechaeum ....B3 XX	
Khaibar............D4 XI	Legio .....C3 XIV, XV, XVI	
Khalman (Aleppo) .....B4 XI		

In this example taken from a real atlas, the maps have been identified with Roman numerals. If you wanted to find Lebanon, you would look at map XXI (21). How many maps in this atlas show the Lebanon Mountains? Did you count six? They are Maps I, XI, XIV, XV, XVI, XX.

This atlas also has much information

about the Bible world. Notice the entry for "Lebanon Mtns." that is in italics. This tells you that you can read about the Lebanon Mountains on page 330.

USING A MAP GRID

Even when a map is indexed, it's impossible to show the exact spot on the map where something is located. However, there is a way to get you close enough to the place that you can find it easily. This is done with a **grid**.

A grid is made of lines running from top to bottom and from left to right over the map, creating squares. The squares going from top to bottom may be lettered (A, B, C . . .). Those going across from left to right would then be numbered (1, 2, 3 . . .). Sometimes it's the other way — the numbers run down the side, and the letters go across the top.

When you looked at the index to find Lebanon, you learned that it was on Map XXI. But there was something else there. The index also gave you a "C3." This is the grid location.

If you could look on Map XXI in that atlas, you could use the grid and find Lebanon. We'll use the sample grid to the right. Find the letter "C" along the top of the page and then look for the number "3" along the side. Follow these rows of squares until they meet. You will be in the square where Lebanon is located. Now look at the names inside that one square until you see the one you want.

The first number given for each entry is the map number. Look at the index for "Jericho." How many maps show Jericho in this atlas? There are two grid numbers for Map 4. That's because there's a small map in the corner of the big map on this page. Those little maps are called **inset maps**. Practice "reading" the map numbers and grid locations in this sample.

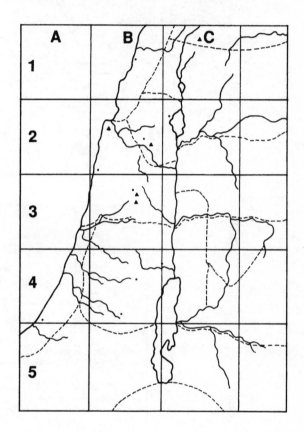

This is a sample taken from a map index in the back of a Bible. Can you "read" it?

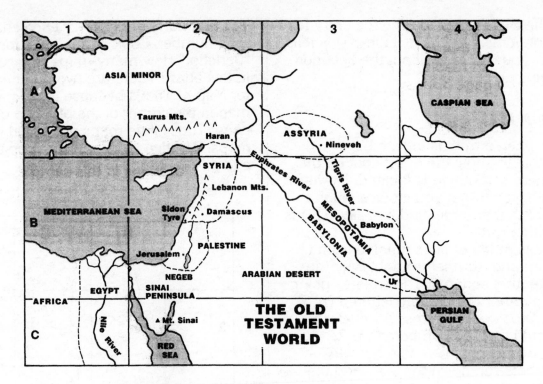

The Old Testament World map showing: ASIA MINOR, Taurus Mts., Haran, ASSYRIA, Nineveh, CASPIAN SEA, SYRIA, Euphrates River, Tigris River, Lebanon Mts., Sidon, Tyre, Damascus, MEDITERRANEAN SEA, MESOPOTAMIA, BABYLONIA, Babylon, PALESTINE, Jerusalem, NEGEB, ARABIAN DESERT, Ur, AFRICA, EGYPT, SINAI PENINSULA, Mt. Sinai, PERSIAN GULF, Nile River, RED SEA, **THE OLD TESTAMENT WORLD**

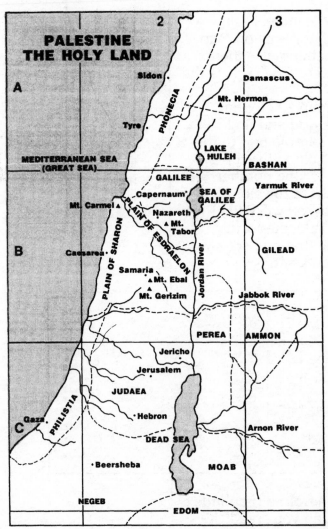

Palestine The Holy Land map showing: PALESTINE THE HOLY LAND, Sidon, Damascus, Mt. Hermon, PHONECIA, Tyre, LAKE HULEH, BASHAN, MEDITERRANEAN SEA (GREAT SEA), GALILEE, SEA OF GALILEE, Yarmuk River, Capernaum, Mt. Carmel, PLAIN OF ESDRAELON, Nazareth, Mt. Tabor, PLAIN OF SHARON, Caesarea, GILEAD, Samaria, Mt. Ebal, Jordan River, Mt. Gerizim, Jabbok River, PEREA, AMMON, Jericho, Jerusalem, JUDAEA, PHILISTIA, Gaza, Hebron, Arnon River, DEAD SEA, Beersheba, MOAB, NEGEB, EDOM

Step 7

The Bible and Me

The Bible and Me

The most important skill of all is yet to be learned. This is the one that will make all the others worthwhile. What you do with this step will affect your entire life. You have learned some skills to help you handle your Bible with confidence. And yet, all of the steps you have taken will be of no value if you don't actually read your Bible. God wants to speak to you through His Word. But you must *want* to know what He's telling you.

This is the time of your life when you're forming the habits that will be with you for a lifetime. If you begin now the habit of reading your Bible every day, you will someday say that it was the best habit you ever made. This step should help you to become a regular Bible reader.

You've seen how important the Bible has been to others through the ages. Some people have given their lives for it. There are people in the world today who are suffering because of the Bible. In many countries it's against the law to own a Bible or to be caught reading it. Parents in those countries aren't allowed to teach their children about God or Jesus or any of the truths of the Bible. Why do some people risk their lives to read it and others hate it? Because it's a very special book. It's actually the Word of God.

BELIEVE IT

If you're studying this book, you must believe in God. If you believe in God, it is probably because you believe the Bible. It isn't enough, however just to *say* you believe the Bible. You must know *why* you believe it. You must believe it's worth the time it takes to study it. If you say that you believe it but never read it, then you *don't* really believe it. Why? Because the Bible itself promises happiness and blessing to those who read it and do what it says. Everyone wants to be happy.

Blessed (happy) are they that hear the word of God and keep it. (Luke 11:28b)

TO TAKE THIS STEP —
Read the Daily Bible Readings and keep the reading record.

HIGH CLIMBERS

Read the Daily Bible Readings AND a Psalm every day.

A LAMP UNTO MY FEET

But he who looks into the perfect law of liberty and continues in it, and is not a forgetful hearer but a doer of the work, this one will be blessed in what he does. (James 1:25 New KJV)

(Other scriptures: Matthew 5:6, John 13:17, John 15:11)

As you grow up, you form opinions of your own about what you believe in and what is important to you. Everyone does. Your parents are trying to help you learn what is right and wrong to help you believe in the right things. Every day of your life, wherever you are, whatever you are doing, you will be making choices based on these beliefs.

Everyone is making choices all the time. Look around you at school, at home, at church, at the store, and you'll see that this is true. In your classroom, some students are choosing to cooperate with the teacher. Others may be breaking rules. Even adults are making choices all the time. At the store, most people will be selecting items and paying for them. A few may be slipping things into their pockets. Jails are filled with people who have *chosen* to break laws.

PEOPLE DO WHAT THEY DO BECAUSE OF WHAT THEY BELIEVE INSIDE.

If everyone makes up his own mind, how can we ever *know* what's really good or bad? If there's no law against something, is it all right to do? What difference does it make if no one else gets hurt — or if you don't get caught? These are the kinds of questions that you must be able to answer.

When you believe the Bible is God's Word to *you*, it will become your own personal guide. It will help you answer such questions. It will give you the beliefs you need inside to help you make the right choices all your life. You must — once and for all — make up your mind to let the Bible teach you what to believe. Then you'll have taken the first step toward pleasing God. (Read Hebrews 11:6.) His image, which was created in you, will begin to grow. You will become a mature, blessed Christian.

BELIEVE IT BECAUSE IT'S FROM GOD

You've already learned that the Bible was inspired by God. As you read it and get to know the stories in it, you'll be more and more sure that it truly is *God's* Word. If you believe this, then you'll be inspired, too, as you read it. You'll listen to Him with your heart, and you'll want to obey what He says.

A LAMP UNTO MY FEET

Yea, rather, blessed are they that hear the word of God, and keep it.
(Luke 11:28b)

BELIEVE IT BECAUSE OF THE PROPHECIES FULFILLED

Many of the events foretold by the prophets have already come to pass. For example, all of the details of His birth were predicted several hundred years before Jesus was born. Events of His life were recorded long before He lived. And yet, the life of Christ fulfilled every one of the predictions. How could these men have known these facts ahead of the time they happened? There have been far too many of them to be able to call it "just **coincidence**." Only God could have known what was going to happen.

If these prophecies have come true, what about all the ones that have not happened yet? Can we believe that they're true, too? Can we expect them to happen just as they're described? Of course we can. And we should take them seriously. We can and should believe every word.

BELIEVE IT BECAUSE IT WORKS TODAY

Have you ever heard someone's testimony? A testimony is given by a person who has had a personal experience. He's a witness that something is true, and he tells others about it. Thousands upon thousands of men and women have testified that the Bible works for them. They have found that believing in and living by the Bible is the only sure way to peace and happiness. For them, it has proved to be the best guide for making decisions.

READ IT

What can the Bible do for you? Absolutely nothing — unless you know what's in it, understand its message, believe it and obey it. And that comes by reading it and hearing it. If you become a regular Bible reader, here are some of the things it can do for you:
— You will get to know Jesus. (II Peter 1:1-12)
— Your mind will be changed to think, like God. (Romans 12:2)
— Your faith will grow stronger. (Romans 10:17)

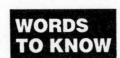 **WORDS TO KNOW**   coincidence (kō IN si dens) — *something which happens by chance.*

— You will prove your love for Jesus. (John 14:21)
— You will be free from fear. (Proverbs 1:32-33)
— You will have joy. (John 15:11)
— You will have peace. (Philippians 4:9)
— You will have health. (Proverbs 4:20-22)
— You will gain knowledge and wisdom. (Proverbs 1:5; 2:6)

BE A WILLING LEARNER

If you want to receive all the blessings in that list, you won't miss any chance to learn the Bible. You'll not only read it for yourself, but you'll listen to those who teach it. Choose the kind of teacher who reads and studies the Bible regularly. Your teacher must also practice its teachings in his or her life. Ask yourself if that teacher is experiencing most of those blessings.

Most churches have classes for all ages. Every time you're in a good class you can learn a little more about some scripture. You may have heard it or read it many times. And yet, you'll learn something new or understand it better each time you hear it again.

PLAN A REGULAR TIME FOR READING

Decide on a time to read your Bible every day. Begin this practice early in your life and early in your day. Try to think of this time as belonging to you and God. Make up your mind that you won't let anything keep you from it. Set your alarm or ask someone to call you 15 minutes earlier than usual. Then, get right up and wash your face. Get your Bible and read for about 15 minutes. You may find it difficult at first, but make yourself do it. After awhile, you should look forward to starting the day with the Lord speaking to you.

If you find that mornings aren't good times for you, then keep trying different times. Perhaps just before you go to bed is best. For many people, this isn't a good time, because it's hard to keep your mind from going over the happenings of the day. Many people find it is hard to stay awake, too. You may want to have your Bible time immediately after school or after the evening meal. The important thing is that it be a time you can do it every day and will not put it off.

HAVE A PLAN FOR READING

Any reading from the Bible can be helpful. However, some scriptures are more helpful than others. What's a good reading plan? Here are several suggestions:

- Sunday School materials and church magazines often give Bible readings for each day of the week. Look for them.
- Decide on a book and read a chapter each day until you finish that book. Then begin another one.
- Read from a book only until you have read a complete teaching or story. Then stop and meditate on it.

MEDITATE ON IT

PRAY BEFORE YOU READ

Before you begin to read each day, ask God to help you understand what you read. Thank Him for His Word. Ask Him to show you how to use it in your own life experiences. This is like getting the soil ready for planting seeds. Hard, lumpy soil will cause seeds to wither and die. The soil must be broken up and softened in order for the seed to start growing. As you pray, you are calling for God's power to help you. This causes your heart to be soft. Then what you read from the Bible will be able to start growing in your life. Little by little, day by day, the things you read will begin to "bear fruit." This means they will become part of what you believe inside. And that will affect all you do and say.

TRUST THE HOLY SPIRIT

If you have prayed, then you can trust Him to help you understand His Word. As you read, keep your mind on what you're reading. Think about it as if it were a letter from God to you. Don't rush or try to read too much at one time. Stop and try to say, in your own words, what you think it is saying to you. Think about God and how much He loves you. Think about how much you love Him. Then try to think of the ways you can please Him. He wants to help you to apply the scripture you have read to your life.

TAKE NOTES

There will be some scriptures you do not understand. But you will still have let God speak to you through His Word. It will be planted inside of you — in your spirit. As you keep reading from His Word day by day, the understandings will begin to come more easily.

When you find a scripture that's especially helpful to you, you may want to mark it in your Bible. It's good to mark the verses you want to remember and practice. Of course, you should try to be very neat and careful. Draw a line under the words of the verse or draw a bracket on each side of it. This makes it easier to find again.

Some people like to take notes about what they read. This is a very good habit. Keep a notebook with your Bible and write down, each day, what you think God is saying to you in that scripture.

THINK ABOUT IT

To *meditate* means "to consider in the mind." *Meditation* means "continued thought." The Word of God is so important that we must think about it over and over and allow its meanings to get deep into our hearts. A good Bible student will want to learn how to meditate on the scriptures he reads.

Here is an example of the kind of meditating all of us do:

Suppose your parents should announce at the evening meal that they were making plans for a family vacation. It might be a camping trip, a ski trip, or a visit to your grandparents in another state. Your mind will begin to go over and over the possibilities of such a trip. *When will we go? What will we do there? Who will I see?* You'll probably tell it to the first person you see and perhaps to all your friends during the day.

This is an example of how you might meditate on a scripture you've read:

Suppose your Bible reading for this morning happened to be Psalm 23: *The Lord is my Shepherd, I shall not want.* Think about this while you brush your teeth and put on your clothes. Your thoughts might go something like this: *What would it be like to be a sheep out in a pasture? My shepherd is watching to see that nothing will harm me. Today He'll see that I have what I need. I'll trust Him and stay close behind Him so that I won't be lost. He'll show me the right paths to follow so I won't get into trouble.*

Later on, during the day, something might happen to spoil your sense of peace. Perhaps another student will suggest a prank that you feel, deep down inside, is wrong. The Holy Spirit may bring to your mind that you have a Shepherd to guide you. Is this the right path for you? Listen to your Shepherd. Those feelings deep down inside are coming out of the scripture that was planted there earlier.

Fill your mind with the scriptures you read. Think about them over and over. As you do this, the truths of God's Word will begin to grow like seeds that have been planted. You'll become what God wants you to be.

LEARN IT

You'll be thankful many times over for every scripture you can quote from memory. Here are a few reasons:

(1) **It helps you in making decisions.**

You need to know what the Bible says about right and wrong if it's going to be your guide. You won't always have a Bible with you when you need to make a decision. Or, you may not know just where to look for the answer you want. If you've memorized parts of the Bible, the Holy Spirit will help you remember just the right scripture verse for the situation.

(2) **You can help others better.**

Many people never read the Bible at all. Even Christians read it very little. If you have memorized verses, when there is a discussion about whether something is right or wrong, you can quote what God's Word says about it. Perhaps it will help someone to decide what is right to do.

When someone you know is sad or lonely or in trouble, you may know just the right verse to tell them to help them feel better.

(3) **It will help you when you need it.**

In times when you are sad or discouraged, there are scriptures that will encourage you. The time may come when you are sick or injured or have to spend some time in bed. The Bible verses you know will give you strength and courage.

Some people live where the Bible isn't allowed. If your Bible were taken away, how much of it could you still have because it's stored in your heart?

Here are some suggestions for memorizing scriptures:

(1) Develop a plan or system for memorizing verses. Choose ones which are especially helpful to you in making choices. Or, select the ones which will help you to know Jesus better.

(2) Always try to learn the reference as well as the words of the verse. You'll be glad that you can remember where it's located in the Bible. That helps you remember some other important things about the scripture: Who said it? Who heard it? What was the meaning in it?

(3) It may help you to write the verse on a small card. Keep the card in your pocket or notebook. Then, you can take it out and work on it whenever you have a few minutes to wait for someone during the day.

OBEY IT

Even after doing all of this, you can still be far from pleasing God with the way you live. You must apply the teachings of the Bible in every situation of every single day. If you know what God's Word says about lying and still tell things that are not true, you cannot be pleasing God.

As you read the Bible, ask God to help you to obey His commandments. If you truly want to please Him, you will *want* to obey Him. When you are tempted to do wrong, He will remind you deep down inside. Then it's up to you whether you give in and do it or not. Jesus said:

If a man loves me, he will keep my word, and my Father will love him, and we will come to him and make our home with him. (John 14:23)

Have you decided that you want to make the Bible your guide book? Have you. decided to read it every day? Then you're ready to start on a lifelong study. By this very decision, you'll be doing one of the things the Bible tells us to do:

Study to show thyself approved unto God, a workman that needeth not to be ashamed, rightly dividing the word of truth. (II Timothy 2:15)

GET STARTED

Look at the SCRIPTURES FOR DAILY BIBLE READING. This gives you some good scriptures to get you started on a Bible reading program. Make a commitment to read the suggested scripture each day for the next 12 weeks. Remember these things as you begin:

1. This commitment is between you and God — not between you and the teacher or anyone else.

2. It's a decision you alone can make.

3. There will be no prize for doing it and no punishment for not doing it. God's blessings are enough.

4. If you fail to read the scriptures for some of the days, don't get discouraged and quit. Go back and read the ones you missed or start where you left off.

5. Keep a record of the scriptures you read.

6. Make yourself write a statement about what you read each day.

You have learned the skills you need to be a good Bible student. You're well prepared to study God's Word. Now get started! Don't put it off! Abide in His Word. Let His Word abide in you. A joyful journey awaits you.

SCRIPTURES FOR DAILY BIBLE READING

WEEK 1	
Sunday	Psa. 23
Monday	Psa. 8
Tuesday	Dt. 6:4-9
Wednesday	Psa. 103:1-14
Thursday	Ex. 20:1-17
Friday	Lev. 26:3-13
Saturday	Mt. 6:5-13

WEEK 2	
Sunday	Prov. 6:20-22
Monday	Rom. 13:1-7
Tuesday	I Jn. 2:7-11
Wednesday	Phil. 2:1-11
Thursday	Zech. 8:16-17
Friday	Isa. 33:15-16
Saturday	Mt. 5:21-24

WEEK 3	
Sunday	Gal. 5:19-26
Monday	Mt. 28:18-20
Tuesday	Psa. 139:1-16
Wednesday	Prov. 1:2-7
Thursday	I Thes. 3:6-13
Friday	Prov. 4:20-22
Saturday	Mt. 5:33-37

WEEK 4	
Sunday	Dt. 8:11-20
Monday	I Pet. 5:7-11
Tuesday	Eph. 4:26-27, 31-32
Wednesday	Psa. 121
Thursday	Mt. 5:27-30
Friday	Prov. 23:29-33
Saturday	Ps. 19

WEEK 5	
Sunday	Mt. 6:25-34
Monday	Isa. 45:22-23
Tuesday	Eph. 6:11-17
Wednesday	John 14:1-6
Thursday	Ecc. 12:12-14
Friday	Jer. 10:1-10
Saturday	Jn. 15:1-7

WEEK 6	
Sunday	Eph. 6:1-3
Monday	Tit. 3:1-3
Tuesday	I Cor. 13
Wednesday	Isa. 40:28-31
Thursday	Psa. 101:1-8
Friday	Mat. 5:38-48
Saturday	I Pet. 3:8-11

SCRIPTURES FOR DAILY BIBLE READING

WEEK 7	
Sunday	Gal. 5:19-26
Monday	Mark 16:15-20
Tuesday	Gal. 3:26-29
Wednesday	Jer. 9:23-24
Thursday	Prov. 24:30-34
Friday	Isa. 53:4-6
Saturday	Mat. 5:33-37

WEEK 8	
Sunday	Mal. 3:8-12
Monday	Psa. 27:1-6
Tuesday	Prov. 29:11, 22
Wednesday	Jer. 17:5-8
Thursday	Eph. 5:1-4
Friday	I Cor. 10:1-14
Saturday	Psa. 84:1-12

WEEK 9	
Sunday	Psa. 86:1-12
Monday	Prov. 30:5-9
Tuesday	Eph. 2:4-10
Wednesday	Mat. 5:17-20
Thursday	Acts 9:36-43
Friday	Heb. 14:12-16
Saturday	Lev. 19:1-3

WEEK 10	
Sunday	I Pet. 2:13-17
Monday	John 13:31-35
Tuesday	Isa. 66:1-3
Wednesday	Prov. 6:16-19
Thursday	Mat. 6:9-15
Friday	Psa. 37:1-9
Saturday	Acts 4:13-22

WEEK 11	
Sunday	Phil. 2:1-13
Monday	Rom. 12:1-3
Tuesday	I Thes. 5:16-23
Wednesday	Jam. 3:1-10
Thursday	Mk. 10:17-22
Friday	Lk. 12:4-7
Saturday	II Tim. 2:23-26

WEEK 12	
Sunday	Isa. 40:28-31
Monday	I Cor. 6:9-20
Tuesday	Dan. 1:10-15
Wednesday	Hab. 3:17-19
Thursday	Jn. 4:1-26
Friday	Col. 1:9-14
Saturday	Mat. 10:32-39

NAME _____

DAILY BIBLE READING RECORD

Tell briefly what you think each scripture is saying to you.   WEEK 1

SUNDAY	DATE	SCRIPTURE	DID NOT READ

MONDAY	DATE	SCRIPTURE	DID NOT READ

TUESDAY	DATE	SCRIPTURE	DID NOT READ

WEDNESDAY	DATE	SCRIPTURE	DID NOT READ

THURSDAY	DATE	SCRIPTURE	DID NOT READ

FRIDAY	DATE	SCRIPTURE	DID NOT READ

SATURDAY	DATE	SCRIPTURE	DID NOT READ

NAME _____

DAILY BIBLE READING RECORD

Tell briefly what you think each scripture is saying to you.   WEEK 2

SUNDAY	DATE	SCRIPTURE	DID NOT READ

MONDAY	DATE	SCRIPTURE	DID NOT READ

TUESDAY	DATE	SCRIPTURE	DID NOT READ

WEDNESDAY	DATE	SCRIPTURE	DID NOT READ

THURSDAY	DATE	SCRIPTURE	DID NOT READ

FRIDAY	DATE	SCRIPTURE	DID NOT READ

SATURDAY	DATE	SCRIPTURE	DID NOT READ

NAME _____

DAILY BIBLE READING RECORD

Tell briefly what you think each scripture is saying to you.   WEEK 3

SUNDAY	DATE	SCRIPTURE	DID NOT READ

MONDAY	DATE	SCRIPTURE	DID NOT READ

TUESDAY	DATE	SCRIPTURE	DID NOT READ

WEDNESDAY	DATE	SCRIPTURE	DID NOT READ

THURSDAY	DATE	SCRIPTURE	DID NOT READ

FRIDAY	DATE	SCRIPTURE	DID NOT READ

SATURDAY	DATE	SCRIPTURE	DID NOT READ

NAME _____

DAILY BIBLE READING RECORD

Tell briefly what you think each scripture is saying to you.   WEEK 4

SUNDAY	DATE	SCRIPTURE	DID NOT READ

MONDAY	DATE	SCRIPTURE	DID NOT READ

TUESDAY	DATE	SCRIPTURE	DID NOT READ

WEDNESDAY	DATE	SCRIPTURE	DID NOT READ

THURSDAY	DATE	SCRIPTURE	DID NOT READ

FRIDAY	DATE	SCRIPTURE	DID NOT READ

SATURDAY	DATE	SCRIPTURE	DID NOT READ

Glossary

anointed —   set apart by God; usually in a ceremony in which oil was poured on the head of that person being anointed.

Apocrypha —   a group of books left out of the Old Testament Canon because they were not considered to be inspired by God; later included in the Catholic Bible.

apostle —   one of the 12 disciples of Jesus; a missionary in the early Church.

archaeologist —   a person who looks for information about ancient people by uncovering the places where they lived.

artifacts —   objects made by ancient people; when found today, they give information about the people who made and used them.

authority —   the power or right to lead people.

Bible reference —   see *Scripture reference*.

canon —   a list of books thought to be inspired by God.

canonizing —   the bringing together of a list of books thought to be inspired by God.

codex —   a manuscript written on parchment sheets and sewn together on the side.

coincidence —   something which happens by chance.

commitment —   a pledge to do something.

concordance —   an index of the important words used in Scripture, giving the reference, thus providing a way to locate the passage.

council —   a group of people called together to settle important questions, usually having to do with church matters.

Council of Jamnia —   a meeting, in A.D. 90, in which the books of the Old Testament were canonized.

Council of Carthage —   a meeting, in A.D. 367, in which the New Testament books were canonized.

covenant —   an agreement between two people or two groups of people.

deacons —   men chosen to look after the physical needs of a local church and its members.

GLOSSARY

Dead Sea Scrolls — copies of Old Testament scriptures found in caves at Qumran near the Dead Sea; oldest copies of scripture available today.

devoted — set apart to serve God only.

disciple — one of the 12 men chosen and taught by Jesus; anyone who learns from a master teacher.

Divided Kingdom — the period in Hebrew history when the 12 tribes separated and formed two nations, Israel (the Northern Kingdom) and Judah (the Southern Kingdom).

elders — men chosen to be the spiritual leaders of a local church.

entries — terms listed alphabetically in a reference; usually in boldface type on the left margin of each page or column.

epistle — a letter; often refers to a book of the New Testament written by one of the Apostles.

Essenes — a group of Jews dedicated to copying the Old Testament scriptures; lived near the Dead Sea at Qumran; hid scrolls in caves.

evangelist — a preacher of the Gospel; usually one who travels.

Exile — the period in Hebrew history when the nation Judah was conquered and her people taken as slaves to Babylonia.

false prophets — men who told the people something and pretended God had said it.

Gentile — any person not a Jew.

grid — a pattern of horizontal and vertical lines forming squares of uniform size on a map, used as a reference for locating specific places.

Gospel — "Good News"; refers to the teachings of Jesus and the Apostles; also refers to one of the first four books of the New Testament.

illuminations — copies of the scriptures that were decorated with pictures and designs.

inset maps — small maps placed within larger ones.

inspired, inspiration — refer to words, ideas, and teachings that come from God.

Israelites — descendants of Israel; another name for Jacob, the grandson of Abraham.

112

judges —   leaders raised up by God to deliver His people from foreign oppressors.

justice —   a fair reward or punishment for something a person has done.

key words —   the most important words in a verse, used as entries in a concordance.

Koran —   a collection of the writings of Mohammed; sacred scriptures to Moslems.

lamentation —   deep sorrow.

Latin Vulgate —   Jerome's translation of the Bible into Latin; the official Bible of the Church for many years.

manuscript —   anything written by hand; often refers to copies of scriptures.

map numbers —   numbers or letters given in a map index to identify the individual maps in that atlas.

Massoretes —   scribes trained to copy the Old Testament scriptures accurately.

meditate —   to consider in the mind; especially, to think seriously about some scripture read.

meditation —   continued thought; usually refers to thinking about spiritual matters.

Messiah —   "the anointed One"; always refers to Jesus Christ.

miracle —   something only God can do.

monarchy —   a country ruled by a king or queen.

monasteries —   places far away from towns where men lived who wanted to serve God only.

monks —   men who wanted to serve God and went to live in monasteries; some gave their lives to the copying of scriptures.

Mosaic Law —   another way to say "the Law of Moses"; refers to the first five books of the Old Testament.

mosque —   a building in which Moslems worship.

papyrus —   an Egyptian plant from which writing material is made and from which we get our word "paper."

GLOSSARY

paraphrase — scripture that has been said in a different way from the original but has kept the original meaning.

parchment — a writing material made from the skins of animals, usually sheep and goats.

pastoral — having to do with the pastor of a church.

Pentateuch — Greek for "five scrolls"; refers to the first five books of the Old Testament.

persecution — hardships suffered by those who remain true to their religious convictions, when to do so is unpopular or unlawful.

Post Exile — the period in Hebrew history which followed the captivity in Babylonia; during this time, Jerusalem and the Temple were rebuilt.

prophet — a man dedicated to God; he spoke God's messages to the people.

psalm — a sacred song or hymn.

proverb — a short, wise saying that expresses a well-known truth or fact.

qualifications — those traits which make a person fit for a job, task, or office.

quill — a pen made of a feather, usually a goose feather.

Qumran — a small community of Essenes, established about the time of Jesus near the Dead Sea; the place where Old Testament scriptures were copied and protected.

reference — a book or source that provides helpful, easily-located information.

related topics — subjects that offer further information about the original one being sought; often listed in reference materials as a help to the reader.

resurrection — coming to life again after having been dead.

revelation — a truth from God that is made known.

ruins — the remains of a fallen building or city.

sacred — belonging to or dedicated to God.

scribe — a person who wrote for another person; also, one who copied scripture.

scriptorium — a place where many men worked at copying scripture.

scripture reference — a notation that gives the name of a book of the Bible with the chapter and verse numbers of a specific passage of scripture.

scroll — a long sheet of writing material, usually papyrus, rolled around two rods.

Septuagint — translation of the New Testament from Hebrew to Greek; probably used in the early churches.

sherds or (shards) — pieces of broken pottery; some give valuable information about the people who made them.

Shrine of the Book — a museum in Jerusalem where the Dead Sea Scrolls are now displayed.

Sinai Codex — a scripture manuscript found in a monastery on Mt. Sinai.

synagogue — a center of worship among the Jews; first established during the Exile.

tell (or tel) — a hill that has been occupied by more than one town, one built on the remains of another.

testament — a covenant; in the Bible, it refers to a covenant between God and man.

testimony — a public statement about one's beliefs or experiences.

theocracy — "rule by God"; refers to the period in Hebrew history when God ruled the people through priests.

tongue — the language of a group of people.

Torah — Hebrew for "the Law"; refers to the first five books of the Old Testament.

translated — changed from one language into another.

tribe — a group of people made up of several generations of a large family, usually living and working together in a community.

uncials — a style of printing, using rounded Greek capital letters.

United Kingdom — the period in Hebrew history when the 12 tribes were one nation, ruled, respectively, by Saul, David and Solomon.

Vatican Codex — contains the oldest known New Testament manuscript and all of the Old Testament; written on vellum in Greek; now in the Vatican Museum in Rome.

vellum — a fine quality of parchment made from the skins of young animals.

GLOSSARY

verse lines —   single lines containing key words, taken from scripture verses and listed in a concordance along with their scripture references; for locating passage in the Bible text.

wadi —   a riverbed that is dry except during periods of rainfall.

wilderness —   a wild forest or desert place; usually not suitable for humans to live.

Worksheets

NAME _____ DATE _____ SCORE_____

OLD TESTAMENT PRACTICE

Can you add the names of the missing books in these boxes?
HIGH CLIMBERS: Spell each name correctly.

Deuteronomy _____

_____

Judges _____

Ezra _____

_____

Esther _____

_____

Psalms _____

_____

Ecclesiastes _____

_____

_____

Ezekiel _____

_____

Hosea _____

_____

_____

Obadiah _____

_____

J _____

M _____

N _____

Habakkuk _____

Z _____

Haggai _____

Z _____

Malachi _____

Genesis _____

_____

Leviticus _____

_____

I _____

II _____

I Kings _____

Job _____

_____

_____

Joel _____

_____

NAME _____ DATE _____ SCORE_____

NEW TESTAMENT PRACTICE

Can you add the names of the missing books in these boxes?
HIGH CLIMBERS: Spell each name correctly.

John _____

_____

Romans _____

_____

_____

_____

_____

_____

Acts _____

II Corinthians _____

_____

_____

Colossians _____

_____

_____

_____

Matthew _____

_____

_____

Hebrews _____

_____

G _____

E _____

P _____

C _____

II Peter _____

_____

_____

II Thessalonians _____

_____

_____

Titus _____

Jude _____

_____

Mark _____

_____

NAME _____ DATE _____ SCORE_____

BOOKS OF THE BIBLE PRACTICE

1. Name the first 5 books of the Old Testament in order:

   _____

   _____

   _____

   _____

   _____

2. Name the books between Joshua and Chronicles:

   Joshua _____

   _____

   _____

   _____

   _____

   I Chronicles _____

3. Name the double books in the New Testament:

   _____

   _____

   _____

   _____

4. Name the first 5 books of the New Testament:

   _____

   _____

   _____

   _____

   _____

5. Name the last 4 books of the Old Testament:

   _____

   _____

   _____

   _____

6. Name the last 2 books of the New Testament:

   _____

   _____

7. Name 2 books of the Old Testament with women's names:

   _____

   _____

8. Name the book between III John and Revelation:

   _____

NAME _____ DATE _____ SCORE_____

ARRANGEMENT OF THE BIBLE
OLD TESTAMENT PRACTICE

1. The order of these division names is scrambled. Can you put them in the right order on the long lines? On the short lines, tell how many books are in each division.

   Minor Prophets _____ _____

   Books of Law _____ _____

   Poetry _____ _____

   Major Prophets _____ _____

   History _____ _____

2. After the name of each book, write the correct name of the division in which it belongs. (They are listed above.) For the Prophets, write only "Major" or "Minor."

   Joshua _____   Exodus _____

   Psalms _____   Hosea _____

   Numbers _____   II Chronicles _____

   Jeremiah _____   Proverbs _____

   I Samuel _____   Esther _____

   Daniel _____   Lamentations _____

3. Name the first book in each of these divisions.

   Poetry _____   History _____

   Minor Prophets _____   Law _____

   Major Prophets _____

4. Name the Books of Law

   (1)_____   (4)_____

   (2)_____   (5)_____

   (3)_____

NAME _____ DATE _____ SCORE _____

 # OLD TESTAMENT PRACTICE
FOR HIGH CLIMBERS

1. How many of the descriptions listed here can you place in the right division of the Old Testament? Read each one and check the proper box on the right.

	LAW	HISTORY	POETRY	MAJOR PROPHETS	MINOR PROPHETS
A. Noah and the Ark					
B. A brave Hebrew queen					
C. Daniel and the lions					
D. Moses as a baby					
E. A fish swallows a man					
F. Songs for temple worship					
G. David's great grandmother					
H. The Battle of Jericho					
I. Creation of the world					
J. Collection of wise sayings					
K. The Ten Commandments					
L. Grief over fallen Jerusalem					
M. The life of Abraham					
N. The time of Samson					
O. Written while in exile					
P. Rebuilding the Temple					
Q. Crossing the Red Sea					
R. Last Prophet of the O.T.					
S. A song about love					
T. Moses' goodbye speech					

2. Can you give three other names for the Books of Law?

(1) _____

(2) _____

(3) _____

3. Can you name the writer of these books?

Psalms _____

Proverbs _____

Genesis _____

NAME _____ DATE _____ SCORE_____

ARRANGEMENT OF THE BIBLE
NEW TESTAMENT PRACTICE

1. These division names are scrambled. Can you put them in correct order on the long lines? On the short lines, tell how many books are in each division.

   History _____ _____

   Prophecy _____ _____

   Gospels _____ _____

   Epistles _____ _____

2. Name the New Testament division in which you would find these books.

   Luke and John _____

   Galatians and Ephesians _____

   Revelation _____

   Timothy and Titus _____

   Matthew and Mark _____

   The Acts of the Apostles _____

   I and II Peter and Jude _____

3. Name the Gospel writers.

   (1)_____ (3)_____

   (2)_____ (4)_____

4. Name the five books written by the Apostle John.

   (1)_____ (4)_____

   (2)_____ (5)_____

   (3)_____

5. Name two letters written by the Apostle Paul.

   (1)_____ (2)_____

NAME _____ DATE _____ SCORE_____

NEW TESTAMENT PRACTICE
FOR HIGH CLIMBERS

1. How many of the descriptions listed here can you place in the right division of the New Testament? Read each one and check the proper box on the right.

	GOSPELS	HISTORY	PAUL'S LETTERS	GENERAL LETTERS	PROPHECY
A. Wise men seek a king					
B. Advice about a runaway slave					
C. The beginning of the Church					
D. Advice to young preachers					
E. Written from prison in Rome					
F. A vision of the end of time					
G. The Messiah is born					
H. Advice to the church in Rome					
I. The teachings of Jesus					
J. Paul's missionary trips					
K. Written from an island					
L. The coming of the Holy Spirit					
M. Written to Hebrew Christians					
N. Advice about the tongue					

2. Identify these letters. Write "Paul" beside the ones written by Paul. Write "General" beside the ones written by others or if the author is uncertain.

Timothy _____   Corinthians _____

Hebrews _____   Thessalonians _____

Jude _____   Philemon _____

Romans _____   Colossians _____

Titus _____   James _____

3. Name the two books written by a Greek doctor.
   (1)_____   (2)_____

NAME _____ DATE _____ SCORE_____

BIBLE REFERENCES
PRACTICE WITH ABBREVIATIONS

I. Give the abbreviations for these books of the Bible.

1. Lamentations _____
2. Ecclesiastes _____
3. Colossians_____
4. Luke _____
5. Nahum _____
6. Timothy _____
7. Haggai _____
8. Ephesians_____
9. Revelation_____
10. Esther_____
11. Hebrews_____
12. Samuel _____
13. Titus _____
14. Kings _____
15. Romans _____
16. Matthew _____
17. Leviticus_____
18. Philippians _____
19. Malachi _____
20. John _____
21. Nehemiah _____
22. Zephaniah _____
23. Hosea_____
24. Micah _____

II. Write the full names of these books of the Bible.

1. Mk. _____
2. Ac. _____
3. Ez. _____
4. Prov. _____
5. Ex. _____
6. Dan. _____
7. Gen. _____
8. Thess. _____
9. Cor. _____
10. Ti. _____
11. Is. _____
12. Nu. _____
13. Gal. _____
14. Sam. _____
15. Chr. _____
16. Zech. _____
17. Hab. _____
18. Jl. _____
19. Jud. _____
20. Dt. _____
21. Phile. _____
22. Josh. _____
23. Ru. _____
24. Jer. _____

NAME _____ DATE _____ SCORE_____

BIBLE REFERENCES
PRACTICE WITH WRITING REFERENCES

Complete this chart by writing the reference correctly in the last column.

	Verses	Chapter	Book	Reference
1.	1 and 12	ten	Proverbs	
2.	1st part of 8	one	Daniel	
3.	11	fourteen	Luke	
4.	17 through 18	nineteen	Leviticus	
5.	last part of 6 through 7	fifty-six	Isaiah	
6.	19 through 25	five	Galatians	
7.	8 and 10	nine	Corinthians, 2nd book	
8.	20 through 21	one	Peter, 2nd letter	
9.	1 through 7	fourteen	Hosea	
10.	21 through 24	five	Amos	
11.	15 through 18	one	Ruth	
12.	3 through 4; 19 through 20	eighteen	Matthew	
13.	last half of 1	three	Ecclesiastes	
14.	12 through 13; 25	twenty-three	Exodus	
15.	9 through 11; 15 through 17	two	John, 1st	
16.	all	one hundred fifty	Psalm	
17.	8 and 9	two	Jonah	
18.	15	——	Obadiah	
19.	all	one	Genesis	
20.	11 through 13	twenty-two	Chronicles, 1st book	

NAME _____ DATE _____ SCORE_____

BIBLE REFERENCES
PRACTICE WITH LOCATION SKILLS

If you were looking for these books in the Bible, in which part would you find them? Write their names where they belong.

1. Exodus
2. I John
3. I Chronicles
4. I Timothy
5. Nehemiah
6. Mark
7. Proverbs
8. Joshua
9. Jeremiah
10. Job
11. Habakkuk
12. Numbers
13. Hebrews
14. Revelation
15. Ruth
16. Joel
17. Judges
18. Isaiah
19. Kings
20. Ezra

First Quarter

Second Quarter

Third Quarter

Last Quarter

NAME _____ DATE _____ SCORE_____

BIBLE REFERENCES
PRACTICE IN READING AND LOCATING REFERENCES

Use these scripture references for practice in reading and locating verses in the Bible. Try to find them as quickly as possible.

A.
Ps. 50:14-15
Zeph. 2:3
Gen. 12:1-2
1 Cor. 4.20
Prov. 13:24
Ob. 15
Dan. 12:3, 10
Psa. 133:1
I Pet. 3:8-12
Prov. 20:11

B.
Lk. 2.11-20
1 Jn. 2.4-6
Eze. 3:27b
Mt. 26:26-28
Phile. 4-6
I Ch. 16:27-29
Gen. 6:6-8
Ezek. 20:18-20
Hos. 6:6
I Cor. 13

C.
Mat. 7:17
Ps. 55.22
1 Tim. 4.12
Re. 22.17
Jno. 4:10-14
Jas. 5.15-16
Tit. 2:11-14
Lam. 3:22-26
2 Pet. 2.19b
Num. 14:7b-9

D.
Mk. 16:15-19
1 Jn. 1.5b, 7
Ecc. 12:1
Jl. 2:12-14a
2 Cor. 7.01
II Sam. 23:3b
II Pet. 1:20-21
Eph. 5:8b-10
Mic. 3:8
Es. 5:6-8

E.
Judg. 21:25
Ja. 4:4
Prov. 3:5-6, 8
1 Tim. 4:7b-8
Zec. 8:16-17
2 Th. 3.3, 5
De. 30.14
Ps. 78:1-4
II Ti. 3:16-17
Rev. 5:12b

F.
Deut. 8:16b-18
3 Jn. 11
Lev. 20:6-9
Josh. 24:15
Ac. 10.34,43
Jde. 20-21
Dan. 4:3
Isa. 54:13-14
Col. 3:20
Eccl. 3:11a

I have looked up and read all the scriptures in

Practice **A** _____   Practice **B** _____   Practice **C** _____

Practice **D** _____   Practice **E** _____   Practice **F** _____

NAME _____ DATE _____ SCORE _____

THE BIBLE'S OWN STORY
PRACTICE

Directions: Match the names and terms with the definitions or descriptions in each box.

1. ____ quill	A.	long sheets of writing material rolled around two rods.
2. ____ parchment	B.	a fine quality of parchment.
3. ____ scroll	C.	a pen made from a feather.
4. ____ papyrus	D.	sheets of writing material attached at the edge.
5. ____ vellum	E.	writing material made from a plant that grows in Egypt.
6. ____ codex	F.	writing material made from the skins of animals.

1. ____ Massoretes	A.	Jews who worked at Qumran to copy and protect Old Testament Scriptures.
2. ____ monks	B.	Those who write or copy for someone else.
3. ____ scribes	C.	Men who took over the copying of the Hebrew Old Testament about 500 years after Christ.
4. ____ Essenes	D.	Men who lived in monasteries.

1. * ____ Latin Vulgate	A.	First Bible to be printed on a printing press.
2. * ____ Septuagint	B.	First Bible divided into chapters and verses.
3. * ____ Wycliffe Bible	C.	Bible decorated with designs and pictures.
4. * ____ Coverdale Bible	D.	First English Bible to be printed.
5. ____ Gutenberg Bible	E.	First Bible translated from Greek to Latin.
6. * ____ Geneva Bible	F.	First translation of the Old Testament into Greek.
7. ____ Illuminated Bible	G.	First Bible translated into English.

1. ____ monastery	A.	A hill where several towns have been built one over the other.
2. ____ scriptorium	B.	Where men live and work to serve God only.
3. ____ Qumran	C.	Where a number of men copy scriptures at the same time.
4. ____ tell	D.	Where the Essenes hid the Dead Sea Scrolls.
5. ____ Shrine of the Book	E.	Museum where the Dead Sea Scrolls are on display for visitors.

* HIGH CLIMBERS

NAME _____ DATE _____ SCORE _____

 # THE BIBLE'S OWN STORY
FOR HIGH CLIMBERS

How much do you remember about the Bible's story? Tell in your own words why Bible students should be grateful for these people.

1. scribes

_____
_____
_____
_____

2. translators

_____
_____
_____
_____
_____

3. archaeologists

_____
_____
_____
_____

4. monks

_____
_____
_____
_____
_____

NAME _____ DATE _____ SCORE_____

CONCORDANCE PRACTICE
READING A CONCORDANCE

Use the sample concordance on page 75 and answer these questions.

1. How many entries are in the first column? _____

2. What is the definition for *servant*? _____

   _____

·3. What does *seraphim* mean? _____

4. How many verse lines are given for *seraphim*? _____

5. Give the first scripture reference for *seraphim* _____

6. What is the first reference to snakes in the Bible? _____
   (Hint: Look under *serpent*)

7. What is the last reference to snakes in the Bible? _____

8. Give a scripture reference about serpents:

   from the book of Proverbs _____

   from the Gospel of John _____

9. What are *sheaves*? _____

10. Give 4 scripture references about *sheaves*. (1) _____

   (2) _____ (3) _____ (4) _____

11. Which scripture reference tells us that Abel was a keeper of sheep?

   _____

FOR HIGH CLIMBERS:

12. Look at the entry word *serve*. How many scripture references
   are from the book of Genesis? _____
   List them: _____

13. Look at the entry word *sheep*. List the references from the
   Psalms: _____

14. How many times does the Gospel of Matthew mention *sheep*? _____
   Give two references from the Epistles about *sheep*:
   (1)_____ (2)_____

NAME _____ DATE _____ SCORE_____

CONCORDANCE PRACTICE
FINDING VERSES

Use your own concordance and practice your skill with these verses. Even if you already know where they are, do each step and fill in the blanks below them.

> *The heavens declare the glory of God;*
> *the firmament showeth his handiwork.*

KEY WORDS (List them)	LISTED (Yes or No)	REFERENCE (If it is given)

> *Jesus saith unto him, I am the way, the truth,*
> *and the life: no man cometh unto the Father,*
> *but by me.*

KEY WORDS (List them)	LISTED (Yes or No)	REFERENCE (If it is given)

NOTES • *Jesus* and *Father* would not be good key words because there would be too many of them in the Bible.
• Since Jesus said it, you know that your reference will be in the Gospels.

Copyrighted ©. Unauthorized reproduction prohibited by law.

147

NAME _____ DATE _____ SCORE _____

CONCORDANCE PRACTICE
STUDYING SUBJECTS

Directions: (1) Choose **one** of these topics and find out what the Bible says about it.

(2) Follow the outline as you study. Fill in as many of the blanks as you can.

*High Climbers: Be prepared to make a talk to the class about your topic. It should be from one to three minutes long.

Topics:
(1) Lying	(6) Studying
(2) Stealing	(7) Going to church
(3) Cursing	(8) Forgiving others
(4) Cheating	(9) Working at a job
(5) Obedience to parents	(10) Killing

MAIN TOPIC: _____

Old Testament References	New Testament References

RELATED TOPIC (1) _____

Old Testament References	New Testament References

RELATED TOPIC (2) _____

Old Testament References	New Testament References

What do you think these scriptures teach us? _____

_____

_____

NAME _____ DATE _____ SCORE _____

CONCORDANCE PRACTICE
FOR HIGH CLIMBERS

Directions: Here are some scripture verses copied from the King James Version of the Bible. Use a concordance (Strong's, Young's Analytical, etc.) to find where they are located. Don't copy the reference until you have looked up the verse in the Bible.

1. Seek ye the Lord while he may be found, call ye upon him while he is near: . . . _____

2. Let all bitterness, and wrath, and anger, and clamour, and evil speaking, be put away from you with all malice. _____

3. And this is the confidence that we have in him, that, if we ask anything according to his will, he heareth us. _____

4. When pride cometh, then cometh shame; but with the lowly is wisdom. _____

5. If ye abide in me and my words abide in you, ye shall ask what ye will, and it shall be done unto you. _____

6. And he said unto them, "When ye pray, say 'Our Father which art in heaven, Hallowed be thy name. Thy . . .'" _____

7. For where envying and strife is, there is confusion and every evil work. _____

8. Upon the first day of the week let every one of you lay by him in store, as God hath prospered him, that there be no gatherings when I come. _____

9. Make thee an ark of gopher wood; rooms shalt thou make in the ark, and shalt pitch it within and without with pitch. _____

10. The heavens declare the glory of God; and the firmament sheweth his handiwork. _____

11. Wherefore, if God so clothe the grass of the field, which today is, and tomorrow is cast into the oven, shall he not much more clothe you, O ye of little faith? _____

NAME _____ DATE _____ SCORE _____

MARGINAL REFERENCES
PRACTICE

JOHN 2   *God So Loved the World*

them all, with the sheep and oxen, out of the temple; and he poured out the coins of the money-changers and overturned their tables. 16And he told those who sold the pigeons, "Take these things away; you shall not make my Father's house a house of trade." 17His disciples remembered that it was written, "Zeal for thy house will consume me." 18The Jews then said to him, "What sign have you to show us for doing this?" 19Jesus answered them, "Destroy this temple, and in three days I will raise it up." 20The Jews then said, "It has taken forty-six years to build this temple, and will you raise it up in three days?" 21But he spoke of the temple of his body. 22When therefore he was raised from the dead, his disciples remembered that he had said this; and they believed the scripture and the word which Jesus had spoken.

23Now when he was in Jerusalem at the Passover feast, many believed in his name when they saw his signs which he did; 24but Jesus did not trust himself to them, 25because he knew all men and needed no one to bear witness of man; for he himself knew what was in man.

3 Now there was a man of the Pharisees, named Nicode'mus, a ruler of the Jews. 2This man came to Jesus*d* by night and said to him,

2.16: Zech 14.21; Lk 2.49
2.17: *Ps* 69.9
2.18: Jn 3.2; 4.48: 6.30;
20.29; Mt 21.23; Mk 11.28: Lk 20.2
2.19: Mt 26.61; 27.40; Mk 14.58:
15.29; Acts 6.14
2.21: Jn 8.57; 1 Cor 6.19
2.22: Lk 24.8; Jn 2.17;
12.16; 14.26; Ps 16.10; Lk 24.26-17; Jn 20.9; Acts 13.33
2.25: Mt 9.4; Mk 2.8; Jn 1.47: 6.61, 64; 13.11; 16.30
3.1: Jn 7.50; 19.39; Lk 23.13; Jn 7.26, 48
3.2: Jn 2.11; 5.36; 7.31; 9.16, 33;
10.38; 14.10-11; Acts 2.22; 10.38
3.3: Mt 18.3; 2 Cor 5.17; 1 Pet 1.23; Mk 10.14-15; Jn 1.13; 3.5;
18.36; Jas 1.18; 1 Jn 3.9
3.5: Ezek 36.25-27; Eph 5.26; Tit 3.5; 1 Pet 1.3
3.6: Jn 1.13; 1 Cor 15.50;
Gal 6.8
3.8: Eccles 11.5; Ezek 37.9; Jn 14.17
3.11: Jn 1.18; 3.32; 7.16-17; 8.26, 28;
12.49; 14.24; 1 Cor 2.14
3.13: Deut 30.12; Prov 30.4; Acts 2.34; Rom 10.6; Eph 4.9;
Jn 3.31; 6.38, 42; 2 Esdras 4.8; Baruch

of the flesh is flesh, and that which is born of the Spirit is spirit.*f* 7Do not marvel that I said to you, 'You must be born anew.'*e* 8The wind*f* blows where it wills, and you hear the sound of it, but you do not know whence it comes or whither it goes; so it is with every one who is born of the Spirit." 9Nicode'mus said to him, "How can this be?" 10Jesus answered him, "Are you a teacher of Israel, and yet you do not understand this? 11Truly, truly, I say to you, we speak of what we know, and bear witness to what we have seen; but you do not receive our testimony. 12If I have told you earthly things and you do not believe, how can you believe if I tell you heavenly things? 13No one has ascended into heaven but he who descended from heaven, the Son of man.*g* 14And as Moses lifted up the serpent in the wilderness, so must the Son of man be lifted up, 15that whoever believes in him may have eternal life."*h*

16For God so loved the world that he gave his only Son, that whoever believes in him should not perish but have eternal life. 17For God sent the Son into the world, not to condemn the world, but that the world might be saved through him. 18He who believes in him is not condemned; he who does not believe is condemned already,

REVISED STANDARD VERSION

This sample from a Bible is from John 2 and 3. List two references for each of these verses. The dots are added to help you find them.

1. John 2:25

_____

_____

2. John 3:5

_____

_____

3. John 3:11

_____

_____

4. John 3:3

_____

_____

5. John 2:16

_____

_____

6. John 2:19

_____

_____

7. John 2:18

_____

_____

8. John 3:1

_____

_____

9. John 3:2

_____

_____

NAME _____ DATE _____ SCORE_____

 # MARGINAL REFERENCES
PRACTICE FOR HIGH CLIMBERS

Directions: For this practice you will need a Bible with marginal references. Read each statement carefully. Then use the marginal references to find the answer.

1. In Matthew 4:4 Jesus quoted a scripture. From what Old Testament scripture was He quoting? Give the reference.

    _____

2. In Acts 8:26-40 there is a story about Philip reading a passage of scripture to an Ethiopian. Read the story and find the Old Testament scripture he was reading. Give the reference.

    _____

3. Read Psalm 24:1. Somewhere in the New Testament this Psalm is quoted. Give the place.

    _____

4. Read Psalm 1:2. Find another place in the Bible where it says almost the same thing.

    _____

5. Read Psalm 23:1. Where does Jesus speak about himself as the Shepherd?

    _____

6. Read Luke 2:1-4. This was prophesied many years before it happened. Who prophesied it? Give the reference.

    _____

7. The Lord's Prayer is found in Luke 11:2-4. Find another place in the Gospels where it is given.

    _____

8. Read John 3:16-17. Find two other references which show that this statement is true.

    _____

    _____

9. Read I Corinthians 13:4-7. If you were making a talk about love, what are some other scriptures you could read on the subject? Get them from the marginal references. Give at least three.

    _____

    _____

    _____

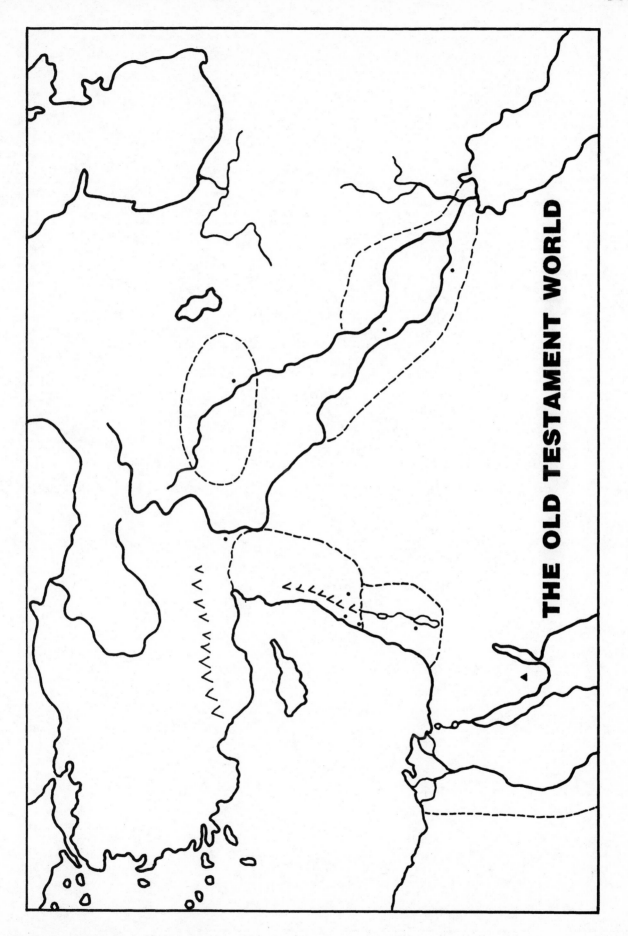

THE OLD TESTAMENT WORLD

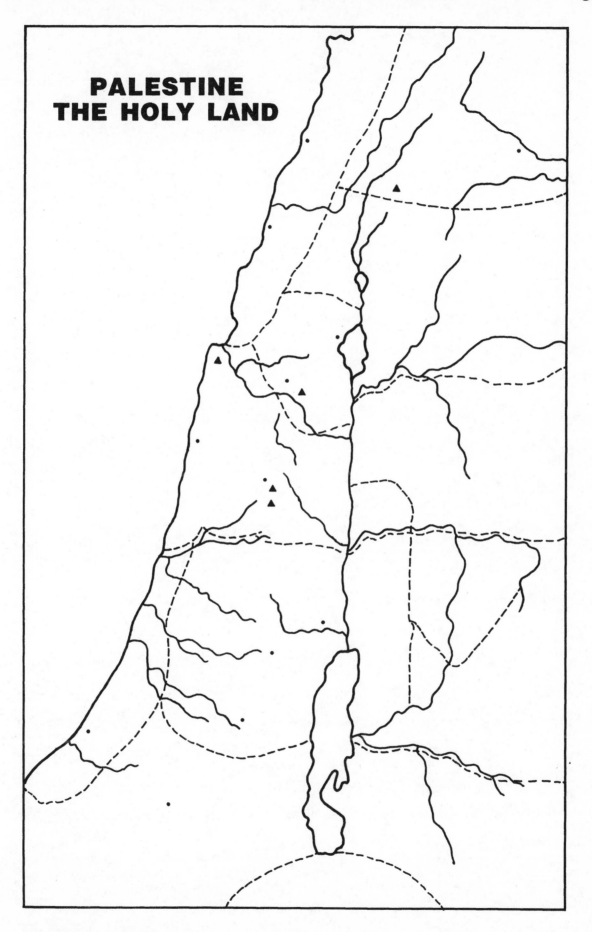

**PALESTINE
THE HOLY LAND**

NAME _____ DATE _____ SCORE_____

OLD TESTAMENT WORLD
MAP PRACTICE

Look up each scripture verse and read it. What place is mentioned in the verse? Write its name in the box beside the reference.

Reference	Place
Am. 1:11	
Gen. 12:4	
Zeph. 2:13	
Ex. 19:20	
Josh. 4:23	
Ac. 7:12	
Dan. 7:1	
Rev. 9:14	
Neh. 7:3	
Gen. 11.28	
Mt. 4:25	
Jon. 3:2	
Lk. 19:1	
Num. 34:12	

Find these places on the Old Testament map, page 96. Give their grid numbers.

1. _____ Assyria
2. _____ Arabian Desert
3. _____ Taurus Mountains
4. _____ Red Sea
5. _____ Haran
6. _____ Sidon
7. _____ Nineveh
8. _____ Negeb
9. _____ Ur
10. _____ Lebanon Mountains
11. _____ Babylon
12. _____ Egypt
13. _____ Damascus
14. _____ Jerusalem
15. _____ Syria
16. _____ Mt. Sinai
17. _____ Mesopotamia
18. _____ Palestine
19. _____ Africa
20. _____ Asia Minor

NAME _____ DATE _____ SCORE_____

PALESTINE
MAP PRACTICE

Look up each scripture verse and read it. What place is mentioned in the verse? Write its name in the box beside the reference.

Reference	Country or Region
II Sam. 10:2	
Ju. 3:8	
Mk. 10:1	
Hos. 6:8	
Am. 2:1	
Mt. 4:12	
Jn. 4:7	
Dan. 7:1	

Reference	City
Lk. 2:51	
Am. 5:5	
Jn. 6:24	
Acts 9:3	
Jos. 19:29	
Mr. 10:46	
I Kgs. 16:29	
Mic. 5:2	

Reference	Mountain
Josh. 8:30	
Ju. 4:6	
Dt. 3:8	
Ex. 33:6	
Dt. 27:12	
I Kg. 18:19	

Reference	River or Sea
Mt. 4:18	
Gen. 32:22	
Ps. 114:3	
Num. 34:6	
Dt. 2:24	
Dt. 3:17	

Find these places on the map of Palestine (Page 96). Give their grid numbers.

1. _____ Mt. Hermon
2. _____ Jerusalem
3. _____ Jordan River
4. _____ Caesarea
5. _____ Phoenicia
6. _____ Samaria
7. _____ Tyre
8. _____ Mt. Carmel
9. _____ Judaea
10. _____ Nazareth
11. _____ Jericho
12. _____ Negeb
13. _____ Dead Sea
14. _____ Philistia
15. _____ Sea of Galilee

NAME _____ DATE _____ SCORE_____

THE BIBLE ATLAS
PRACTICE

Study this sample from a map index. Fill in the chart below with the correct information from the index. Some boxes will be empty.

```
Perga ......................... IV -E 2        Safed. See Haifa .............. III -B 3
Pergamos. See Pergamum ......... IV -D 2       Saida. See Sidon ......... III-C 1; IV -F 3
Pergamum (Pergamos) ............ IV -D 2       Salamis ...................... IV -E 2
Perizzites .................... II -B 2        Salem. See Jerusalem .......... II -B 3
Petra. See Sela ............... I  -C 2        Salonica. See Thessalonica ....... IV -C 1
Pharpar River ................. III -E 1       Salt Sea. See
Phenice. See                                      Dead Sea ...... II-B 3; III-C 5-6; IV -F 3
   Phoenicia ............ III-C 2; IV -F 3      Samaria (city) ...... II-B 2; III-C 4; IV -F 3
Phenicia. See                                  Samaria (country) ............... III -C 4
   Phoenicia ............ III-C 2; IV -F 3      Samos ........................ IV -D 2
Philadelphia (Alashehr) ........ III -D 4      Samothrace (Samothracia) ......... IV -C 1
Philadelphia (Asia) ........... IV -D 2        Samothracia. See Samothrace ....... IV -C 1
Philippi ...................... IV -C 1        Sardis ....................... IV -D 2
Philistia ............... I-C 2; III -B 5      Sarepta. See Zarephath ......... III -C 1
Philistines ................... II -A 3        Scythopolis .................. III -C 3
Phoenicia (Phenice) ........ III-C 2; IV -F 3  Sea of Chinnereth. See
Phoenicians .................. II -B 1            Sea of Galilee .............. III -D 3
Phrygia ...................... IV -D 2         Sea of Galilee .............. III -D 3
Piha-hiroth (Bir-Suweis) .......... I  -B 2
```

NEW ANALYTICAL BIBLE

	Map Number	Grid Location	Map Number	Grid Location	Map Number	Grid Location
Phoenicia						
Sea of Galilee						
Samaria (Country)						
Samaria (City)						
Philistia						
Dead Sea						
Philippi						
Salamis						
Philadelphia (Asia)						
Pergamum						
Salonica						
Samos						
Safed						

NAME _____ DATE _____ SCORE _____

THE BIBLE ATLAS
PRACTICE FOR HIGH CLIMBERS

Study this sample from a map index. Fill in the chart below with the correct information from the index. Some boxes will be empty. Note: Some grid locations are the same on more than one map. Give only two map numbers for these.

Lachish, *T. ed-Duweir.* 8:A6; 10:D4; 11, 12, 14, 15, 19, 38:W6; 13:G6
Ladder of Tyre, *Ras en-Naqura.* 23, 26, 27, 28:X3
Lagash, *Telloh.* 9:K4
Laish, (Dan), *T. el-Qadi.* 8:B3; 11:Y3
Lambesis. 36:C4
Laodicea, *Eskihisar,* in Asia Minor. 37:G4
Laodicea, *Lattaqieh,* in Syria. 31, 37:H4
Larissa. 32, 33:A1; 36:F3
Larsa, *Senkereh.* 9, 16:J4
Lasea, near Fair Havens, Crete. 33:C5
Lebanon, mts. and region. 4, 11, 12, 14, 19, 23, 25, 26, 28:Y2; 8:C3; 13:H4; 31:H5
Lebanon, nation. 39:E1
Lebanon, Cedars of, grove. 39:E1
Lebo-hamath, *Lebweh.* 13:H4

Marah, *'Ain Hawarah* (?). 10:B6
Marathon. 18:A2
Mareshah, (Marisa), *T. Sandahanna.* 12, 15, 19, 23, 38:W6
Margiana, *Merv.* 18:F2
Margus, region. 18:E2
Mari, *T. el-Hariri.* 9:H3
Mariamne Tower, in Jerusalem. 29
Marisa, (Mareshah), *T. Sandahanna.* 23, 26:W6
Masada, *es-Sebbeh.* 23, 25, 26, 28, 34, 35, 38:X7; 39:E4; *see also plan p. 34, illust. p. 34*
Massagetae, people. 18, 20:F1
Massalia, (Marseilles). 21, 22:B1
Mauretania, region. 22:A1; 36:B4
Mawjib, Wadi. 39:E4
Medeba, *Madaba.* 12, 14, 15, 19, 23, 25, 26:Y6; 13:H6
Medes, (Madai), people. 16:K3
Media, region. 9:K3; 17, 18, 20:D3

Nahal Hever, (Cave of Letters). 34:X7
Nahal Se'elim. 34:X7
Nahariyah. 38:X3
Nain, *Nein.* 26, 27, 28:X4
Naphtali, tribe. 11:X3
Narbata, Narbartah, *Kh. Beidus.* 19, 23, 25, 26, 35:X4
Naucratis. 37:G5
Nazareth, *en-Nasireh.* 4, 25, 26, 27, 28:X4; 39:D2
Neapolis, *Kavalla,* in Macedonia. 32, 33:A1
Neapolis, *Nablus,* in Palestine. 26, 28, 35:X5
Neballat, *Beit Nabala.* 19:X5
Nebo, *Nuba,* in Judah. 19:X6
Nebo, Mt., *Jebel en-Neba.* 4, 11, 15:Y6; 10:E3
Negeb, *Negev,* region. 4, 11, 12, 15:W8; 8:A7; 10:D4; 39:D4
Nehemiah's Wall, in Jerusalem. 18

HAMMOND'S ATLAS OF THE BIBLE LANDS

	Map Number	Grid Location	Map Number	Grid Location	Map Number	Grid Location
Mount Lebanon						
Lachish						
Nazareth						
Media						
Negeb						
Laodicea						
Marathon						
Nain						
Mount Nebo						
Masada						